CAD/CAM OF DIES

ELLIS HORWOOD SERIES IN MECHANICAL ENGINEERING

Series Editor: J. M. ALEXANDER, formerly Stocker Visiting Professor of Engineering and Technology, Ohio University, Athens, USA, and Professor of Applied Mechanics, Imperial College of Science and Technology, University of London

The series has two objectives: of satisfying the requirements of postgraduate and mid-career engineers, and of providing clear and modern texts for more basic undergraduate topics. It is also the intention to include English translations of outstanding texts from other languages, introducing works of international merit. Ideas for enlarging the series are always welcomed.

CAD/CAM OF DIES

J. S. GUNASEKERA

Ph.D., M.Sc., D.I.C., M.A.S.M.E., M.A.I.I.E, M.I.Mech.E., M.I.Prod.E., M.I.E.(Aust.), M.I.E.(S.L.)
Moss Professor of Mechanical Engineering
Ohio University, Athens, USA

ELLIS HORWOOD LIMITED
Publishers · Chichester

Halsted Press: a division of
JOHN WILEY & SONS
New York · Chichester · Brisbane · Toronto

First published in 1989 by
ELLIS HORWOOD LIMITED
Market Cross House, Cooper Street,
Chichester, West Sussex, PO19 1EB, England
The publisher's colophon is reproduced from James Gillison's drawing of the ancient Market Cross, Chichester.

Distributors:

Australia and New Zealand:
JACARANDA WILEY LIMITED
GPO Box 859, Brisbane, Queensland 4001, Australia

Canada:
JOHN WILEY & SONS CANADA LIMITED
22 Worcester Road, Rexdale, Ontario, Canada

Europe and Africa:
JOHN WILEY & SONS LIMITED
Baffins Lane, Chichester, West Sussex, England

North and South America and the rest of the world:
Halsted Press: a division of
JOHN WILEY & SONS
605 Third Avenue, New York, NY 10158, USA

South-East Asia
JOHN WILEY & SONS (SEA) PTE LIMITED
37 Jalan Pemimpin # 05–04
Block B, Union Industrial Building, Singapore 2057

Indian Subcontinent
WILEY EASTERN LIMITED
4835/24 Ansari Road
Daryaganj, New Delhi 110002, India

© **1989 J. S. Gunasekera/Ellis Horwood Limited**

British Library Cataloguing in Publication Data
Gunasekera, J. S. (Jay S.). *1946–*
CAD/CAM of dies.
1. Dies. Design and manufacture. Applications of computer system
I. Title
621.9'84

Library of Congress CIP available

ISBN 0–7458–0636–8 (Ellis Horwood Limited)
ISBN 0–470–21404–X (Halsted Press)

Printed in Great Britain by Hartnolls, Bodmin

CHAPTER 8 FUTURE OF CAD/CAM OF DIES

Die design and manufacturing for metal forming has an industrial history spanning more than a few centuries. During the last 25 years, as a result of spectacular technological advances, the economical importance of metal-forming processes, associated die design and manufacturing processes has increased considerably. The computer has become the key element in the integration of design, analysis, and manufacturing functions.

CAD/CAM has found a wide range of applications in all areas of engineering, design, and manufacturing. While the developments and applications of CAD/CAM technology in certain areas have been wide-spread, its application in other areas, such as die design and manufacturing, has been fairly limited.

This book is an expanded version of two monographs which the author and some of his colleagues have been requested to write for the ASM and SME Handbooks. It contains the latest technology in CAD/CAM of dies based on the experience of the authors and on the most important recent publications in this area.

The book is intended to provide a comprehensive introduction to this complex subject of the CAD/CAM of dies for those in industry, R & D organizations and universities, with particular reference to advances in materials technology, analytical modelling, and computers and graphics technology. It will provide valuable, detailed information to both undergraduate and graduate students as well as researchers in this field and may well be used as a text for special courses in CAD/CAM, materials technology, and die design and manufacturing technology.

This book could not have been completed without the collaboration of many acknowledged experts, in particular the process modelling group of Dr. H. L. Gegel of the U.S. Air Force Materials Laboratory, Wright-Patterson Air Force Base, Dayton, Ohio. Special thanks are due to Dr. Sokka Doraivelu, Technical Director, Universal Energy Systems, and Messers James Malas, James Morgan, and Richard Kavaulaskas, Air Force Wright Aeronautical Laboratories, WPAFB, for their assistance and cooperation in the areas of analytical and physical modelling. Thanks are also due to my past and present students both from Australia and the U.S.A., associates in my company — Super Technology International, in particular Research Associates Amer Ali and Anis Ahmed, and Bhavin Mehta, Manager Intergraph CAD System at Ohio University, who have made valuable contributions to the material in this book.

A book of this nature could not have been completed without the research and development efforts of various scientists and engineers throughout the world. In that connection, I wish to mention the following additional names and organizations who in my opinion have contributed most to the advancement of the CAD/CAM dies: Dr. Taylan Altan, Battelle Columbus Laboratories (presently at Ohio State University); Prof. K. K. Wang, Cornell University; Dr. W. Knight, Oxford University, U.K., (presently with University of Rhode Island); Dr. John Berry, Georgia Institute of Technology; Drs. R. Davis and H. Siauw, Manufacturing Technology Division, CSIRO, Australia, and their respective research groups.

Finally, it would have been impossible for me to complete this book without the constant encouragement and help of my former supervisor, Professor John M. Alexander at Imperial College, U.K., and the understanding of my wife, Mal and daughters, Manisha and Upendri. I dedicate this book to my parents, Mal, Manisha, Upendri, and Professor Alexander.

Jay S. Gunasekera
Moss Professor of Mechanical Engineering
College of Engineering and Technology
Ohio University
ATHENS, Ohio 45701-2979, U.S.A.
15th Sep. 1988

Chapter 1

INTRODUCTION AND GENERAL PRINCIPLES

1.1 Computers and CAD/CAM

Computers first appeared in the 1940's. The early inventions were bulky, cumbersome to use and performed computations rather slowly in comparison to modern digital computers. They advanced from mechanical relays to vacuum tubes to transistors to silicon chips. Computers today are more compact, faster and less expensive than their predecessors. Today some microcomputers can handle the computations of early day main-frames. Technological advances in this field have been truly dramatic.

The application areas of computers have also grown rapidly. Computers are widely used in the fields of Engineering, Business, Education and Medicine. However, the most spectacular growth has been in the area of CAD/CAM – Computer Aided Design and Computer Aided Manufacture. This new technology, which emerged within the last decade or so, has helped to increase Engineering productivity tremendously. Higher productivity is probably the primary consideration that influences most potential users to acquire a CAD/CAM system. CAD/CAM provides the integration of design, analysis and manufacturing functions into a system which is available to the user at his fingertips. In addition, other routine and monotonous (but important) tasks such as the preparation of bills of materials, costing, production scheduling, etc. may be performed automatically using the same computer network. Another major benefit in the use of CAD/CAM is reduced lead time from concept to design to manufacture. Product development cost can also be reduced dramatically because analysis such as the finite element method can be interfaced with design to arrive at the optimum design within a very short time.

CAD/CAM and Analysis are best used in an interactive, computer graphics environment to provide solutions to engineering problems as illustrated in Fig. 1.1. The geometry and topology of the part and other parameters such as material properties are stored in a common data base which can be accessed by any one of the functions. Analysis such as finite element methods, upper bound methods and slab analysis is carried out on the initial product geometry.

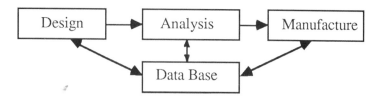

Fig. 1.1 Interactive computer graphics environment

Results which are often displayed in colour will either automatically or with user interventions alter the design parameters so as to satisfy the various design criteria. This process is repeated until an optimum solution is obtained. Thereafter manufacturing and other related functions can be performed either automatically or with user intervention.

1.2 CAD/CAM System

Any CAD/CAM system consists of hardware, such as the central processing unit (CPU), disk storage facilities, display units, tablets, etc. and software, which is the brain behind the system. Sometimes it is harder to make a clear distinction between the two, when hardware is built-in with appropriate software. This is often referred to as "firmware."

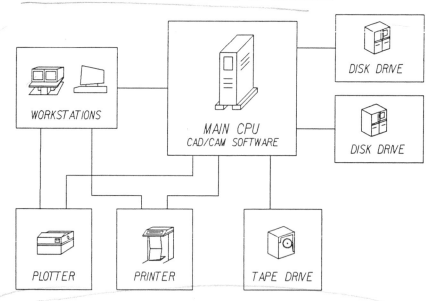

Fig. 1.2 Typical CAD/CAM system configuration

Fig. 1.3 Typical CAD/CAM work station
(Courtesy of Intergraph Corp.)

A typical CAD/CAM system configuration is illustrated in Fig. 1.2. The heart of the system is the central processing unit (or the computer), which coordinates all the functions within the CAD/CAM system. The user interacts with the system through the work station. A typical work station is shown in Fig. 1.3. It consists of a graphic display (or two, as in this case) which provides visual output of the system to the user. The user can communicate with the system through the keyboard or a tablet (with menu) as shown in Fig. 1.4. The dual-screen work-station has numerous advantages. It can be used to view the product being designed at two or more angles. The zoom command may be used to zoom up a certain feature of the product on one screen for detail view while the other screen can be used to view the whole part. Text may be entered on any one of the screens. Other vendors have systems with graphic display and an alpha-numeric display for text.

The work stations (Fig. 1.5) are intelligent, in that they do useful local operations such as zoom, rotate, etc, without tying up the CPU for these operations. The current trend is to increase the power of the work station, thus freeing the CPU for other more demanding tasks. Many CAD/CAM systems have a "menu" of commands to choose from a tablet or digitizer board. The menus can be changed depending upon the applications. Some CAD/CAM systems use a push-button menu to select certain commands. A typical menu used in a CAD/CAM system is shown in Fig. 1.6.

Fig. 1.4 Typical CAD/CAM tablet with menu

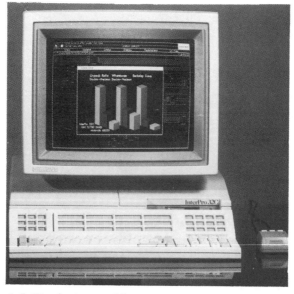

Fig. 1.5 Typical graphic and alpha-numeric displays
(Courtesy of Intergraph Corp.)

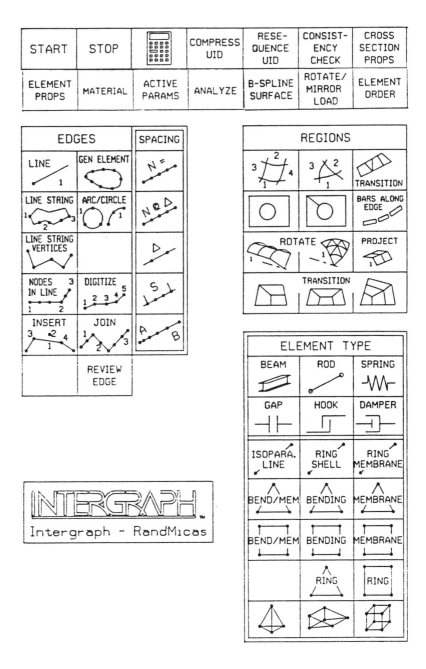

Fig. 1.6 Typical CAD/CAM menu
(Courtesy of Intergraph Corp.)

1.3 Die Making

Die making has been an art more than a science. The design and manufacture of dies have been passed down for decades from die and tool designers and tool makers to their apprentices and so on. This process is undergoing some revolutionary changes with the advent of computers, CAD/CAM technology and powerful analysis such as the finite element method. Details of these will be presented in the following chapters of this book.

Dies for processes such as hot forging, extrusion, casting, and plastics moulding are usually produced by manual machining, copy milling or by electric discharge machining (EDM). In the conventional EDM process the electrode is frequently manufactured by copy milling from a suitable pattern. EDM is particularly useful for die manufacture as it can be employed for intricate shapes in hard-to-machine materials. Most of the common methods used in die making involve highly skilled time-consuming manual operations. The use of CAD/CAM for die making has substantial benefits, as will be demonstrated in the following chapters.

The dies considered in this book for CAD/CAM and analysis fall into the following categories:-

a)   Hot forging dies for metals
b)   Hot extrusion dies for metals
c)   Cold extrusion dies for metals
d)   Die casting dies for non-ferrous metals
e)   Sand casting dies for ferrous metals
f)   Polymer extrusion dies
g)   Plastics moulding dies

However, because of the author's personal experience with hot extrusion dies for metals, detailed discussion (design, analysis and manufacturing) will be limited to these dies. Because of the similarity of the analysis and manufacturing (and some design) functions, the techniques presented here are equally applicable to most of the types of dies mentioned above.

Chapter 2

MANUFACTURING PROCESSES AND CONVENTIONAL DIE DESIGN

2.1 Introduction

Dies and moulds are used in a variety of manufacturing processes. By far the largest use has been in the manufacture of discrete parts using metals and plastics. Manufacturing using dies and moulds offers numerous advantages over other manufacturing methods such as machining and joining processes. (When medium to large production runs are involved, moulding and forming methods become superior in terms of lower unit costs and better mechanical properties. Material utilization is very high with most processes utilizing dies and moulds. If proper processing conditions are maintained, rejection rates become very low.) Production rates are usually very high and overall high productivity of the manufacturing operation can be achieved.

There are inherent advantages of the extrusion and forging processes of making discrete parts. Fundamentally, these processes shape metals under high pressure. This controlled deformation of material (usually performed at elevated temperature) results in metallurgical soundness and improved mechanical properties. The following advantages are specifically for the extrusion and forging processes, but some may well equally apply to other manufacturing processes considered here:

*Superior mechanical properties
*Ability to process modern heretofore "unprocessable" materials such as P/M alloys and fibre reinforced composites.
*Extreme reliability
*Closer tolerance capabilities
*High strength
*Structural integrity
*High impact and fatigue resistance
*High uniformity
*Wide range of sizes
*Wide range of materials

*Low rejection rates
*Economy of machining
*High material utilization

This chapter provides detailed descriptions of the extrusion process and of the concepts of conventional die design. Other manufacturing processes and associated die designs are also briefly mentioned.

2.2 Extrusion Process and Die Design

Extrusion is a metal forming process in which a billet is forced to flow through a die to form a product of uniform cross-section along its length. The billet is usually of circular cross-section, whereas the desired product may have any shape for its cross-section. There are two common types of extrusion dies, viz.:-

(i) the so-called "flat-faced" or "shear" die which is commonly used in the extrusion of aluminium; and

(ii) the "shaped" or "converging" die which has found applications in the lubricated extrusion of titanium, nickel and steel alloys (Fig. 2.1).

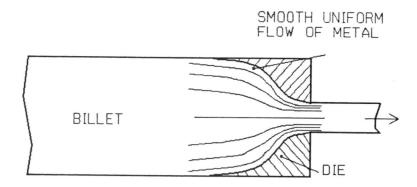

SMOOTH UNIFORM
FLOW OF METAL

BILLET

DIE

Fig. 2.1 Shaped extrusion die

A variety of aluminium alloys (the 1000 to 7000 series) are extruded conventionally through flat-faced dies and have a wide variety of both commercial and military applications. Amongst all these alloys, the high-strength aluminium alloys (the 2000 and 7000 series) are those most widely used for aircraft applications. Other alloys, such as 1100, 3003, 6061, 6062, 6063, and X6463, are used for manufacturing goods for a variety of applications, such as construction, household applications and transportation[1].

2.2.1 *The Extrusion Process*

The two most significant extrusion processes for aluminium are direct and indirect extrusion, and these are illustrated schematically in Fig. 2.2. With aluminium, lubricant is not normally used[1]. The extrusion method, which uses no lubrication between the billet, the container, and the die, is used to produce complex shapes with excellent surface finish and close-dimensional tolerances. These shapes are considered to be "nett" extrusions and they are generally used in the as-extruded form, after necessary straightening and surface-coating operations[2].

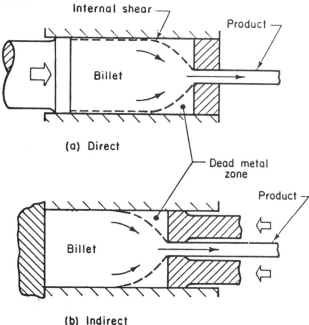

(a) Direct

(b) Indirect

Fig. 2.2 Direct and indirect extrusion, with internal shearing
(after NAGPAL and ALTAN[4])

In non-lubricated extrusions of aluminium, the billet is extruded through a flat-faced (or shear) die. As the pressure is applied to the end of the billet, internal shearing occurs across certain planes within the billet, and fresh metal is forced out through the die orifice. This fresh metal accounts for the bright finish obtained on extruded aluminium shapes. With this technique, however, very high extrusion forces are required because of internal shearing between the flowing and the stationary metal along the container surface and at the die corners (Fig. 2.2). The energy dissipated by internal shearing, or redundant work, represents energy that is converted into heat, and results in a gradual increase of the product temperature as the extrusion proceeds. If not controlled, this adiabatic heating can be sufficient to cause hot shortness and melting in the extruded material[2].

2.2.2 *Extrusion Speed and Temperatures*

In order to increase the production rate in extrusion, it is desirable to achieve as high an extrusion ratio as possible. Therefore, with hard aluminium alloys, the maximum possible billet preheat temperatures are utilized. This combination of high extrusion ratio, high starting billet temperature, and the dangers of overheating due to redundant work, necessitates very low extrusion speeds for extruding a sound product. Thus, a ram speed of 1/2 in/min is quite common. With a typical extrusion ratio of 40:1, exit speeds of the extrusion can be in the order of 2 to 4 ft/min. Fig. 2.3 shows the range of extrusion exit speeds used for different aluminium alloys[3]. It is of interest to note that for soft alloys the speeds are reasonably high; however, for hard alloys, such as 2024 and 7075, extrusion rates are quite low. Consequently, the use of lubrication in extruding high-strength alloys can be expected to increase the extrusion rate and to reduce extrusion costs. However, lubrication does not offer any significant advantages in extruding the soft alloys[4].

By far the greatest proportion of all aluminium extrusion consists of heat-treated alloys and all of these have a critical temperature associated with the presence of low-melting intermetallic compounds that restrict the permissible extrusion temperatures, as pointed out by CHADWICK[5]. Because of the slow speed of extrusion, the tooling temperature is maintained close to (about 50 to 100°C below) that of the billet, so that chilling of the billet is minimized. AKERET[6] conducted theoretical and practical studies of temperature distribution in the extrusion of aluminium alloys under conditions in which the container and tools were initially below, equal to, or above the initial billet temperature. He deduced that, for the particular experimental conditions employed, the rise of temperature under adiabatic conditions should be about 95 °C. For practical purposes, it can be estimated that, in extruding high-strength alloys, the maximum temperature rise likely to be encountered will not exceed 100 °C. For the soft alloys where lower specific extrusion pressures are required, the product temperature under normal production conditions is not likely to exceed 50 °C[5]. LAHOTI and ALTAN[7,8] at Battelle's Columbus Laboratories have developed computer programs to predict temperatures in the extrusion of rods and tubes from various materials.

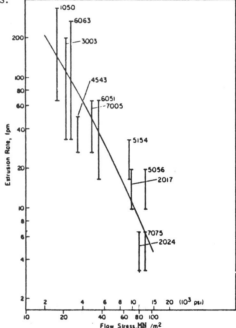

Fig. 2.3 Range of extrusion speeds used for aluminium alloys[3]

As seen in Fig. 2.4, based on theoretical predictions as well as on experimental evidence, the product temperature increases as extrusion proceeds.

The temperature at the product surface is higher than the temperature at the product centre. This is illustrated in Fig. 2.5 for given extrusion conditions. Thus, it is seen that the surface temperature of the product may approach the critical temperature where hot shortness may occur, only towards the end of the extrusion cycle. The temperature of the extruded product, emerging from the die, is one of the essential factors influencing the product quality. Therefore, an ideal procedure for establishing the maximum speed of extrusion at all times would be to measure this temperature and to use it for controlling the ram speed. This procedure was proposed in an early patent by MUNKER[9], but the problem of obtaining an accurate and continuous temperature measurement of the extruded product remains unsolved. Methods for measuring the product temperature by using various types of contact thermocouples, or by radiation pyrometry, did not prove to be practical.

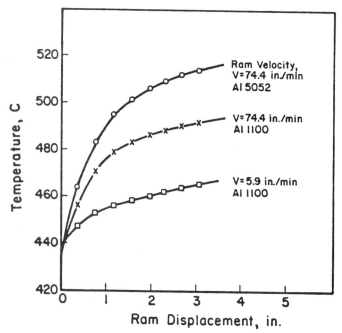

Fig. 2.4 Variation of product temperature during extrusion[7]

LAUE[10] was the first to propose a system for isothermal extrusion in which the ram speed variation, necessary to keep the product temperature within the required limits, was pre-established. In presses, designed to operate on this principle, the working stroke is divided into zones, each having a preset speed. In a press used for extruding the high-strength alloys, a saving of 60 per cent in time was claimed. This saving would certainly be less in the case of more easily extruded alloys. According to FERNBACK[11], to make full use of the isothermal-extrusion principle, it would be necessary to pre-

determine, by trial and error, a large number of speed
programs for extruding different alloys and products.

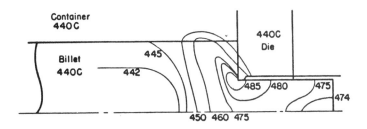

(a) Ram displacement = 0.75 in.

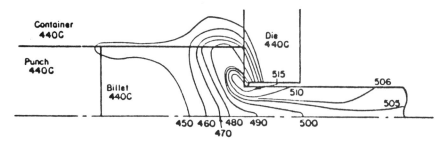

(b) Ram displacement = 3.7 in.

Fig. 2.5 Temperature distribution across extruded product[7]

The intense shearing taking place inside the conventional
shear (or flat-faced) die causes uneven generation of heat
within the material which results in the uneven temperature
distribution across the section shown in Fig. 2.5. This short-
coming of the shear die is overcome to a certain extent by
the use of streamlined dies, as will be demonstrated in later
sections.

2.2.3 *Dies for Conventional Aluminium Extrusion*

There are four general designs of flat-faced dies for
extruding aluminium, as shown in Fig. 2.6:

   (a)   solid-shape
   (b)   porthole
   (c)   bridge
   (d)   baffle or feeder-plate

The solid-shape dies are primarily used for extruding solid shapes. These dies are made by machining an opening of the desired shape in the die block as shown in Fig. 2.6(a). The porthole die design, shown in Fig. 2.6(b), has porthole openings in the top face of the die from which material is extruded into two or more segments, and then, beneath the surface of the die, welded and forced through the final shape configuration to form a part. The tubular portion of the extruded shape is formed by a mandrel attached to the lower side of the top die segment. This provides a fixed support for the mandrel and a continuous hole in the extruded part. Fig. 2.6(b) also shows typical complex parts that can be made through the use of a porthole type arrangement.

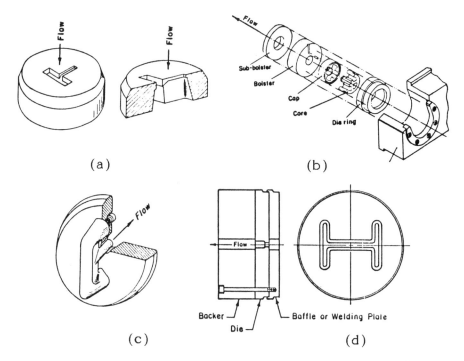

(a)   (b)

(c)   (d)

Fig. 2.6 Flat-faced extrusion dies:- (a) solid-shape[12],
(b) porthole[14], (c) bridge[12], (d) baffle or welding-plate[13]

Bridge dies are quite similar to the porthole dies and are also used for extruding hollow products. The "bridge" which divides the metal extends into the container, as shown in Fig. 2.6(c). Compared to porthole dies, bridge dies are less rigid. However, the removal of the extrusion, left in the container at the completion of the extrusion cycle, is more difficult with porthole dies than with bridge dies.

Another interesting type of die design, shown in Fig. 2.6(d), is the so-called baffle or feeder-plate die, which is used to serve several purposes. The feeder plate provides a uniform feed of metal into the cavity of the die, which induces flow control and assists in maintaining the contour of the extruded section. It also permits the next billet to weld itself partially to the material in the cavity, ensuring a straight run-out for the next extrusion. This method helps to extrude straighter extrusions and to reduce scrap. These feeder plates are used for single and multi-hole dies of all sizes and shapes. Other die designs used for specific products have been described by DEBUIGNE[13] and BELLO[14].

In conventional unlubricated extrusion with flat-faced dies, the material always shears against itself and forms a dead, or stationary, zone at the die face (Fig. 2.2). The formation of the dead zone minimizes the overall rate of energy dissipation, but in general does not give, in extrusion of shapes, uniform metal flow at the die exit. Non-uniform metal flow can result in twisting and bending of the emerging product. To prevent this, the flow rate is controlled through proper design of the die land and by proper positioning of the die cavity with respect to the billet centre, as discussed by MOCKLI and LOCHER[15].

2.2.4 Die-Land Design and Correction

There is a general agreement that longer die lands improve the tolerances and straightness of the extruded products. However, the extrusion load increases with increasing length of the die land. Thus, the die land must be designed to give a uniformly strained product within desired tolerances and without excessive extrusion pressure.

In lubricated cold-rod extrusion, KEEGAN[16] gives some approximate rules for estimating the land length in dies. WILSON[17] and FELDMAN[18] also recommend certain land lengths. SIEBER[19] suggests that in axisymmetric extrusion, there is an optimum land length which is given by the following equation:

$$L_e = 1.2d \text{ to } 0.8d \qquad (2.1)$$

where:-

L_e = land length
d = land diameter.

In shape extrusion, unlike in rod or tube extrusion, the die land length is changed to slow down or to speed up metal flow. According to BELLO[14], with shear-faced dies, the flow can be enhanced by filing a relief bearing or can be slowed down by filing a choke surface on the die land, as seen in Fig. 2.7.

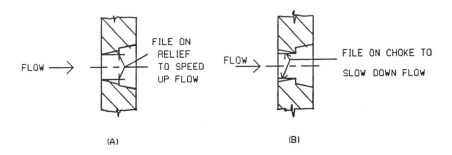

Fig. 2.7 Modified die land for control of extrusion flow[14]

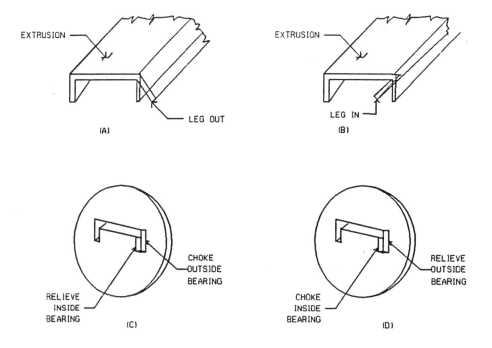

Fig. 2.8 Modified die land to control extruded product shape[14]

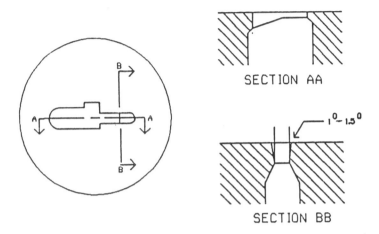

SECTION AA

SECTION BB

Fig. 2.9 Varying die land in accordance with
section width to control flow[20]

The shape of the extruded section can be modified by
filing choke and relief on the die land, as shown in Fig. 2.8.
In Fig. 2.8, the metal at the outside of the right leg flows
faster than that inside.   Therefore, with the die-land
corrections indicated in Fig. 2.8, the right leg will tend to go
toward the inside.   A similar but reverse situation exists in
Figs. 2.7b and 2.8.
In the practical design of the die land for extrusion of
aluminium shapes, the land is varied in length according to
section width, in order to obtain uniformity of flow.   As
described by CHADWICK[20] and shown in Fig. 2.9, the thin
section is provided with less land than the thicker section.
An empirical guideline is to keep the land length equal to 1
to 2 times the section thickness[15].   Another empirical relation,
proposed by Matveev and Zhuravski as described by
PERLING[21], is to make the effective length of the die land,
at the various portions of the die opening profile, inversely
proportional to the specific perimeters of these portions, as
follows:-

$$\frac{l_m}{l_n} = \frac{P_{sn}}{P_{sm}}$$

$$P_{sm} = \frac{P_m}{A_m} \qquad (2.2)$$

$$P_{sn} = \frac{P_n}{A_n}$$

where l_m, P_m, A_m, P_{sm} =   effective land length, perimeter, cross-sectional area, and specific perimeter, respectively, of the portion "m" in the die profile.

l_n, P_n, A_n, P_{sn} =   effective land length, perimeter, cross-sectional area, and specific perimeter, respectively, of portion "n" of the die profile.

"m" and "n" are any two portions of the die profile which have different cross-sectional thicknesses.   When die land length is assigned to a specific portion of the profile, the land length at other portions of the profile can be determined by using Equation 2.2.

2.3 Forging Processes and Die Design

Forging is one of the most important manufacturing operations.   It is a plastic deformation process similar to extrusion but, unlike extrusion, it can be used to manufacture complex 3-D parts.   Forging can be classified into three main categories:- open-die forging, impression-die forging and closed-die forging.

2.3.1 Open-Die Forging

The process is schematically illustrated in Figure 2.10. At least one of the workpiece surfaces deforms freely, and hence the open-die forging process produces parts of lesser accuracy and dimensional tolerance than impression-die or closed-die forging.   However, the tooling is simple, relatively inexpensive and can be designed and manufactured with ease.

2.3.2 Impression-Die Forging

This forging process is schematically illustrated in Figure 2.11.   It can be used to produce complex 3-D shapes having a greater accuracy than closed-die forging.   The specially manufactured dies contain the negative of the forging to be produced.   In one form of the process, the shape is obtained by filling the die cavity formed by the upper and lower dies. Excess material is allowed to escape into the flash.   There may or may not be special provision for flash formation.

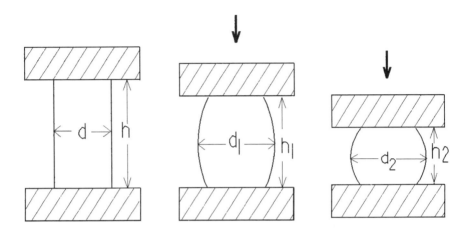

Fig, 2.10 Illustrating open-die forging

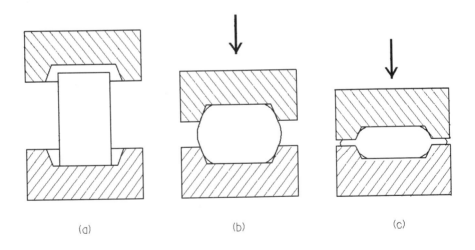

(a)   (b)   (c)

Fig. 2.11 Illustrating impression-die forging

These dies are illustrated in Figures 2.12 and 2.13.

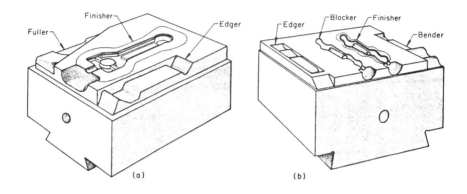

Fig. 2.12 Dies for closed-die forging[22]
(Courtesy of ASM)

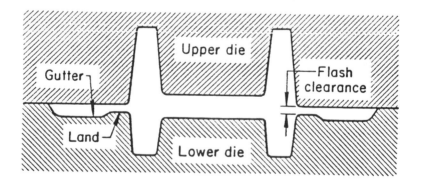

Fig. 2.13 Section through a forging-die finisher impression[22]
(Courtesy of ASM)

The die cavity must be filled without defects. A complex shape cannot be filled completely without defects in one operation starting with a rectangular or cylindrical shape. Some preforging steps are necessary to ensure complete filling of the dies without defect formation. The preforging or preforms can be produced in other forging operations such as open-die or in the same die with different die cavities, or by other processes such as rolling or roll-forging.

The preform may be further shaped to bring it closer to the final configuration in a "blocker die," which ensures proper distribution of material within the die. Excess material is allowed to run out between the dies into a flash. Before forging in the finishing die the excess material may be removed in a trimming die. A thick flash in the finishing die means high pressure within the die, which assures proper die filling. Excessive pressure may break dies or reduce their life, and some control on this may be exercised by proper control of the flash land.

The geometry of the preform and the forging dies must promote smooth material flow. Therefore, a parting line is chosen with proper consideration of the fibre structure of the finished forming. After the parting line is located the die walls are given sufficient draft to permit removal of the forging from the die cavities. Fillets and corners must be given appropriate radii to ensure smooth material flow and long die life.

2.3.3 Closed-Die Forging

In closed-die forging the workpiece is completely trapped in the die and no flash is generated. Material utilization is very high, but the volume of the workpiece before and after forging is identical and hence control of incoming material volume becomes critical. Excess material can create large pressures, which are liable to cause die failure.

2.3.4 Die Manufacture

Conventional die manufacture is more of an art than a science. Several alternatives are available for impression die manufacture. The common methods are conventional milling, copy milling, electric discharge machining (EDM) and electro-chemical machining (ECM). Dies may also be cast from special tool steels.

REFERENCES

(1) *Aluminium Extrusions, Fabricating and Anodizing.*
Booklet published by Southern Extrusions Inc., Arkansas.

(2) BYRER, T.G. *et al.* "Design Guide for the Use of
Structural Shapes in Aircraft Applications",
Battelle's Columbus Labs. Technical Report
AFML-TR-73-211, September 1973.

(3) AKERET, R. and STRATMAN, P.M., "Unconventional
Extrusion Processes for the Harder Aluminium Alloys",
Parts I and II, *Light Metal Age* April 1973, pp. 6-10 and
June 1973, pp. 15-18.

(4) NAGPAL, V. and ALTAN, T., "Computer-Aided Design
and Manufacturing for Extrusion of Aluminium, Titanium
and Steel Structural Parts", (Phase 1),
AVSCOM Report No. 76-12, *Battelle Columbus Labs.,* 1976.

(5) CHADWICK, R., "Developments and Problems in Package
Extrusion Press Design",
Metals and Materials May 1969 pp. 162-170.

(6) AKERET, R., "A Numerical Analysis of Temperature
Distribution in Extrusion", *J. Inst. Metals* 1967, **95**, 204

(7) LAHOTI, G.D. and ALTAN, T., "Prediction of Metal
Flow and Temperatures in Axisymmetric Deformation
Processes", *Proc. 21st Sagamore Army Materials Research
Conf.*, 1974.

(8) LAHOTI, G.D. and ALTAN, T., "Prediction of
Temperature Distributions in Tube Extrusion using a
Velocity Field without Discontinuities",
Proc. 2nd N.A.M.R.Conf. 1974, pp. 209-204

(9) MUNKER, T., German Patent No. 901,529, 1953.

(10) LAUE, K., "Isothermal Extrusion", (in German),
Z.Metallkunde 1960, **51**, 491.

(11) FERNBACK, H.R., "Programmed Speed-Control Methods
for the Extrusion Process",
J. Inst. Metals 1963-64, **92**, 145-148.

(12) VAN HORN, K.R., (Ed.), *Aluminium, Vol.3, Fabrication
and Finishing*, A.S.M., Metals Park, Ohio, 1967, pp.
81-132.

(13) DE BUIGNE, C., "Design and Manufacture of Aluminium
Extrusion Dies", *Light Metal Age* 1969, 27, 28-33.

(14) BELLO, L., *Aluminium Extrusion Die Correction.* Fellom
Publications, San Francisco, 1973

(15) MOCKLI, F. and LOCHER, M., "State of the Art in Making Extrusion Dies", (in German), *Aluminium* 1965, **41**, 629.

(16) KEEGAN, J.W., "Hints in Modern Cold Heading", *Automatic Machining* 1966, **28(2)**, 63-66.

(17) WILSON, G., "Cold Forging", *Metal Treatment* 1966, **33(252)**, 345-353.

(18) FELDMANN, H.D., *Cold Forging of Steel.* Hutchinson and Company, Ltd., 1961.

(19) SIEBER, K., "Special Cold Forging Tools, Particularly for Solid Forming on Multi-Stage Transfer Presses", *Wire World International* 1964, **6(6)**, 165-178.

(20) CHADWICK, R., "The Hot Extrusion of Nonferrous Metals", *Metallurgical Reviews* 1959, **4(15)**, 189-255.

(21) PERLIN,I.L., *Theory of Metal Extrusion.* Metallurgia, Moscow, 1964. (English Translation FTD-HT-23-616-67).

(22) Metals Handbook - Forging and Casting, eighth edition, American Soceity for Metals, 1980, **5**, 21-22.

Chapter 3

MODERN MATERIALS TECHNOLOGY

3.1 Introduction

Modern materials play an important role in our lives. They range from ferrous metals to non-ferrous metals to ceramics and plastics. Research into new non-metal composite materials and fibre reinforced metal matrix composites has highlighted some of these materials possessing improved properties and low cost.

Manufacturing is the process by which raw materials and semi-finished products are transformed into goods and articles. The designer selects materials to satisfy certain performance criteria. The criteria may be certain physical, chemical or mechanical properties (such as electrical and thermal conductivity or strength) or shape and size. These performance criteria have to be satisfied, however, at a cost which is competitive. Because the raw material costs are usually a fraction of the overall costs of an article or product, the selection of the material should be made in conjunction with selection of the appropriate manufacturing process.

Metals have been the most widely used engineering materials. However, recent developments in metals and the increasing sophistication of many products have shifted, somewhat, the major role of metals in manufacturing.

3.2 Mechanical and Physical Properties of Materials

There are a number of properties that determine the suitability of a given material for a manufacturing process. The strength of the material is commonly the most important one. Strength affects the ease with which it can be shaped and also its final ability to resist loads during service. Ductility is another property which is beneficial for some manufacturing functions. Ductility is the ability of a material to undergo large plastic deformation without fracture. The choice of the material and the manufacturing process is influenced by properties such as strength and ductility. Much of the knowledge in this area has come from empirical formulae and trial-and-error methods. For instance, it is well known that heating a metal makes it softer and easier to deform. However, this benefit is lost if the speed of deformation is too great.

There are also several physical and chemical properties which influence the selection of materials and manufacturing processes. For example, thermal conductivity will affect the flow of heat within the material being deformed. Properties such as strength-to-weight ratio and stiffness are important selection criteria in the aircraft industry.

3.3 Standard Mechanical Tests

Standard mechanical tests are used to determine the mechanical properties of a material which can then be used during the selection procedure. A list of standard mechanical tests is given below. For details the reader should refer to any textbook on materials.

a)   tensile
b)   hardness
c)   creep
d)   fatigue
e)   impact
f)   compression

Of these, the compression test is widely used to determine either the work hardening or strain-rate hardening behaviour of materials subjected to large strains and elevated temperatures. This test is used to determine the constitutive behaviour of metals which is then used in modelling the process, as in the finite element method, for example.

3.4 Modern P/M Technology

Powder Metallurgy (P/M) is a relatively new area of interest in process engineering (see GEGEL *et al.*[1]). Over the past 25 years, most of the information in the literature has been devoted to studies of powder-making processes for difficult-to-form materials, cold compaction techniques for producing near-nett-shape compacts, and the sintering processes. The recent development of P/M alloys and the advent of Rapid Solidification Technology (RST), however, has demanded hot-consolidation and subsequent plastic working to ensure the required shape and mechanical properties. Therefore, the P/M process — as it is understood today — can be divided into three general areas:- (1) powder making, (2) preform or blank making (consolidation), and (3) plastic working of blanks or preforms. Although this is a simplistic breakdown of a complex process (aside from the final operations), it is sufficient to provide an overall perspective. An issue in P/M technology that can be influenced by these processing steps leading to the finished part is that of <u>economics</u>. Each step in the P/M process is important because defects which occur during these steps generally cannot be removed by sintering or heat treatment. Therefore, the objectives of this section are (1) to examine P/M processing from the vantage-point of a vendor (forging or extrusion industry, Fig. 3.1), and (2) to present some recent results of deformation process modelling which was conducted for the purpose of improving the properties of RST P/M materials in a finished part.

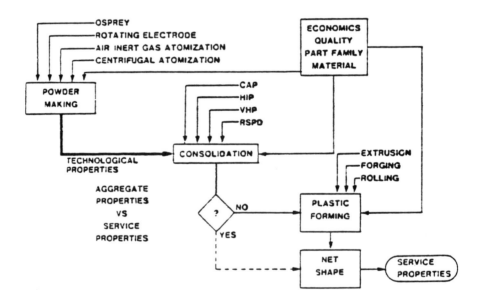

Fig. 3.1 P/M processing as seen by the vendor[1]

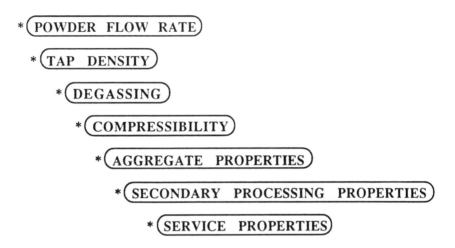

* POWDER FLOW RATE
* TAP DENSITY
* DEGASSING
* COMPRESSIBILITY
* AGGREGATE PROPERTIES
* SECONDARY PROCESSING PROPERTIES
* SERVICE PROPERTIES

Fig. 3.2 Technological properties of consolidated powders[1]

SERVICE PROPERTIES

- YIELD STRENTH
- ULTIMATE TENSILE STRENGTH
- DUCTILITY
- TOUGHNESS
- LOW CYCLE FATIGUE
- HIGH CYCLE FATIGUE
- HIGH TEMPERATURE PROPERTIES

PLASTIC WORKING PROPERTIES

- INTERPARTICLE BOND STRENGTH
- RELATIVE DENSITY
- CONSTITUTION
- WORKABILITY

Fig. 3.3 Aggregate properties of consolidated powders[1]

3.4.1 *Powder Making*

In the P/M process, the powder-making step is of the utmost importance because the fundamental powder characteristics of the individual particle such as composition, size, shape, microstructure, and surface structure are controlled by the particular process used to produce the particles. These powder characteristics, in turn, control the technological properties, especially the aggregate properties of the consolidated materials which are listed in Figs. 3.2 and 3.3.

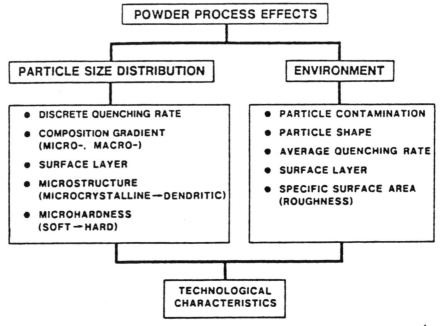

Fig. 3.4 Effects of particle characteristics on the P/M process[1]

Several popular powder-making processes which are being investigated as possible methods for making RST powders are:- air atomization, centrifugal atomization plus forced convection, helium-gas cooling, the rotating electrode process, and the Osprey process. Although other processes exist, they will not be discussed here. The powder produced by each of these processes has its own distinct characteristics. Two of the factors most strongly influencing the subsequent sequences of any P/M process are (1) particle size distribution and (2) the environment, which controls the average cooling rate. Other important factors are – as shown in Fig. 3.4 – particle shape, particle contamination, surface layer, and specific surface area.

The particle size distribution controls the discrete cooling rate of each particle and hence determines which of the particles will be quenched to the micro-crystalline and which to the dendritic structure. Therefore, particle size controls the final hardness, composition gradient, surface layer, and micro-structure. A range of microstructures is usually found for the alloy powders produced by the various processes. It has been observed that the centrifugal-atomization process usually produces a more narrow size range, as shown in the study conducted by HILDEMAN *et al.*[2] on the Al-Ni-Fe alloy system (see Fig. 3.5). This can be an advantage in cases where it is necessary to have a controlled-microstructure distribution.

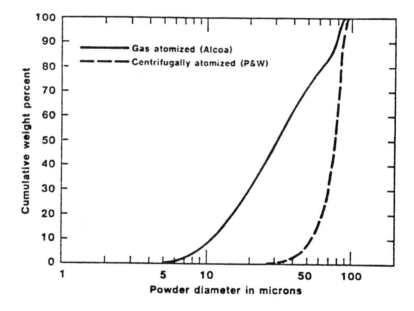

Fig. 3.5 Particle size range found in Al-Ni-Fe
system using centrifugal-atomization[1]

Alloy systems designed for high-temperature applications, which contain strong intermetallic compounds, present some unique difficulties because of the wide range of micro-structures which develop as a result of the discrete quenching rate for each particle associated with a particular particle size distribution. A large difference in the temperature dependence of the micro-hardness value is expected for particles having the micro-crystalline structure and those having the dendritic

structure.   From studies investigating the LCF behaviour of
nickel-based P/M materials, it is known that the interfaces of
coarse particles of dendritic structure are sites for fracture
initiation.   It has been observed that some critical strain is
required to ameliorate the difficulties associated with the
coarse powders and foreign matter introduced by powder
handling.   Overcoming these effects is a metal-working
problem which could be simplified if it were possible to work
only with powder having a homogeneous microstructure as well
as chemical composition.   The coarse dendritic particles retain
their hardness with increasing temperature; therefore, they
behave as rigid bodies, moving with the metal flow pattern.
They do not shear and often agglomerate, which exacerbates
the problem.   The metal-working problem then is to control
the distribution and strengthen the matrix to permit the
transfer of stress and strain into the dendritic particles.   The
latter is required to condition the particles in such a way that
they will be energetically favourable for recrystallizing during
subsequent processing steps.

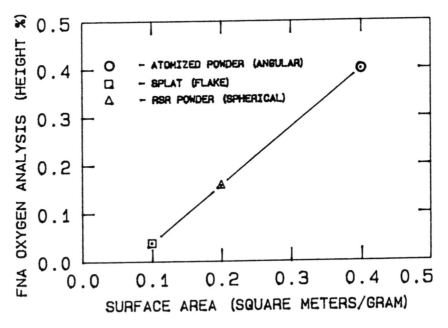

Fig. 3.6 Variation of oxygen content with surface area
for different shapes of Al-Ni-Fe alloy powders[1]

The surface layers of metal-alloy powders are enriched
with impurities; therefore, the physical properties may differ

considerably from those of the base material. This layer may
be enriched with some solute element, an oxide layer, a
hydrated oxide layer, a metallic carbide, an intermetallic
compound, or a combination of these, e.g. an oxide layer plus
an intermetallic compound. The surface compositon is
controlled by the size arfd shape of the particle since both
affect the specific surface area. As an example, HILDEMAN
et al.[2] showed the variation of oxygen content with surface
area for angular, flake, and spherical Al-Ni-Fe alloy powder
(see Fig. 3.6). The powder-making process controls the nature
of the surface layer and the physical properties of the base
material. The surface layer is an important part of the
particle structure since it accepts the contact load when the
powder is poured into the mould.

The contact pressures on the surface layer, due to the
small surface area or particle contact area, become so great
that either plastic deformation or local fracture of the particle
occurs. The stress state of the particle is always at some
limiting or critical value, and the surface layer in the contact
zone will either deform plastically or fracture. The most
general orientation of the contact load during the compaction
process is a combination of normal and tangential loads. The
surface layer is always perturbed by the inter-particle contact
loads. Surface layers with hydrated oxide films are of particular importance to aluminium alloys made by air atomization
using RST. These layers must be converted to some stable-
oxide form before subsequent processing steps can be initiated.
During this conversion process, the volatile components are
liberated over different temperature ranges, as shown by MSA
and TGA studies. The results are presented in Figs. 3.7 and
3.8 for X7091 aluminium powder.

Failure to make this conversion will lead to a phen-
omenon known as blistering which occurs when the above
volatile components are liberated during subsequent thermal
exposures. This problem can be solved for certain aluminium
powders by subjecting them to a suitable degassing treatment.
In Fig. 3.8, degassed and VHP compacts show little liberation
of any volatile matter up to 400°C. However, around 500°C,
magnesium and zinc are volatilized and liberated. Therefore,
a proper degassing temperature should be selected to avoid loss
of these elements for this particular alloy. Nickel-base alloys,
in contrast, should not be allowed to form a stable oxide on
their surface because this acts as a site for heterogeneous
nucleation of a γ' surface for these alloy systems. Inert
powder-making and powder-handling systems should be used

for this class of alloy system.

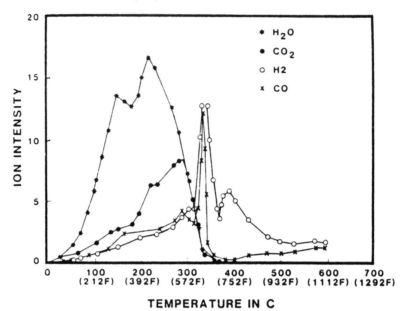

Fig. 3.7 Results of MSA and TGA studies
on X7091 aluminium powder[1]

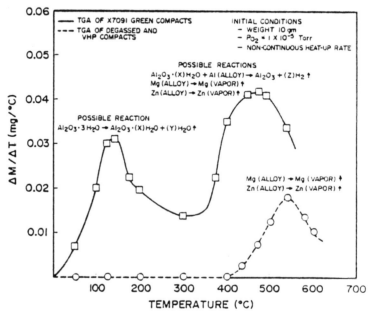

Fig. 3.8 Results of MSA and TGA studies
on X7091 aluminium powder[1]

3.4.2 *Consolidation*

The preform or blank-making process is controlled to a
large extent by the powder-making process and also by the
physical properties of the individual particles.   A powder
compact before application of external pressure consists of
many physical particles which are more or less uniform in
composition.   The particles range in size from fine to coarse,
and their corresponding microstructures range from micro-
crystalline to coarse dendritic.   At tap density, these powders
usually retain their shape, and they can exert pressure on the
surrounding medium.   However, they cannot resist tensile
stresses.   The compact at tap density occupies a position
somewhere between a liquid and a solid.   The technological
characteristics of this powder, as listed in Fig. 3.2, depend
upon the resistance of the individual particles to compression,
shearing, and bending.   The high-temperature RST aluminium
and nickel-base P/M alloys have considerable resistance to
these types of loading.   The higher the hardness of the
particle and the greater its surface roughness, the lower the
tap density for the powder compact.   Correspondingly, the
punch must travel a greater distance in the case of low tap
density, which results also in higher tool wear.

The properties of this compact continuously change during
pressing.   Individual particles are linked together by different
bonds which depend upon the dimensions of the particles.
The bonds are usually between individual particles in contact
with other particles and the bonding is due to adhesion at the
contact surfaces. Particles which are soft and plastic form
strong adhesion bonds during cold compaction, while those
which are hard and less ductile do not.   A practical
comparison can be made between the cold compaction of
X7091 which is a soft, ductile aluminium alloy and the cold
compaction of Al-8Fe-4Ce which is a high-hardness alloy.
The latter composition cannot be ejected from a simple
cylindrical mould when cold compacted without severely
cracking, while the former material develops excellent green
strength and can be ejected as a cylinder under similar
conditions.

The compacting pressure tends to cause the particles to
shift and occupy the most stable geometric position; this is
accompanied by contact distortion and shearing of the particles.   The basic particle shape tends to remain undistorted.

Angular particles, relative to spherical particles, do not form better green-strength compacts since green-strength is principally controlled by the strength of local adhesion. Vacuum hot pressing (VHP) or hot isostatic pressing (HIP) must be used to densify a compact when the particles are hard and resist compression. The aggregate properties of the compacts produced by VHP or HIP should be equivalent to the service properties of the components. Otherwise, these compacts demand subsequent forming operations which are explained in detail in the following section. In this case, the aggregate properties of the billet should be at least equivalent to the plastic-working properties.

3.4.3 *Plastic Working*

Plastic working of P/M preforms is recently being used increasingly in powder metallurgy as a means of shaping and strengthening the finished part. Plastic working has been observed to improve markedly the properties and microstructures of finished shapes by decreasing the residual porosity, increasing the strength of the matrix, and imparting a better surface finish. Additionally, controlled plastic working of preforms or billets is now being considered as a means of strengthening and increasing their workability. This additional working is also thought to be essential for controlling the properties in the finished shape. The results of many empirical observations indicate that a critical strain is required to overcome the effect of large particles and foreign debris which are introduced during powder handling. Parts forged directly from an untreated preform or billet often do not receive sufficient plastic deformation and improper strain distribution often leads to increased scatter and reduced values of these critical mechanical properties.

Plastic working is essential for overcoming powder-making defects such as discrete foreign particles and size-distribution-related defects. To perform proper plastic working on P/M material, it is essential to obtain a good understanding of the material behaviour during plastic shaping. This understanding necessitates the development of a plasticity model for porous bodies which satisfactorily describes the experimental results. While the problems involved in the plastic working of P/M materials have much in common with those of conventional alloys, a number of differences exist which are the direct result of the discrete nature of the individual powder particles. One important feature of the plastic deformation of a porous body is that it undergoes a permanent change in volume, which affects its Poisson's ratio [ZHDANOVICH[3]; KUHN[4]]. Another characteristic is that the mechanical strengthening experienced by a porous solid during plastic deformation is brought about not only by a change in porosity but also by strengthening of the matrix.

A continuum-mechanics approach is being used for modelling different P/M metalworking processes using the finite-element method (FEM) for obtaining solutions. This requires a plasticity theory applicable to porous materials and constitutive equations with density as one of the parameters for studying densification during deformation, as explained below.

3.4.4 Plasticity Theory – Porous Material

The design of billet-consolidated processes and of the dies used to forge or extrude porous P/M materials to full density requires a special yield function for development of the plasticity analysis. The plastic-flow behaviour component of stress influences the onset of plastic flow. The effect of hydrostatic stress is taken into account by adopting a yield function of the form:-

$$AJ_2' + BJ_1{}^2 = Y_R{}^2 = \delta Y_0{}^2 \qquad (3.1)$$

Here, J_2' is the second invariant of the deviatoric stress, and J_1 is the first invariant or the hydrostatic component of the total stress. Y_0 and Y_R are the yield stresses of fully dense and partially dense materials, respectively. A, B, and δ are functions of the relative density.

Many researchers have determined these constants through heuristic arguments and by using experimental results. GREEN[5] presented an analytical method which considered a uniform cubic array of spherical voids in a solid under states of stress corresponding to pure shear and hydrostatic compression. The results for these two stress states allowed determination of the two variables A and B in Equation 3.1. He assumed the stress distribution to be uniform in two directions through the minimum section of the array and the effect of the voids on the stress in the third direction to be negligible on the planes midway between the voids. OYANE et al.[6] determined A and B using more stringent assumptions. They found poor agreement between their theoretical and experimental results and, therefore, reported experimentally determined values in a later paper. SHIMA and OYANE[7] abandoned this analytical approach entirely and, instead, refined empirical relations obtained from their experimental values. KUHN and DOWNEY[8] also presented experimentally obtained values for these two variables. However, DORAIVELU et al.[9] derived these variables taking into account the distortion energy due to the total stress tensor. The final equation obtained was:-

$$(2+R^2)\ J_2' + \frac{(1-R^2)}{3}\ J_1{}^2 = (2R^2-1)Y_0{}^2 \qquad (3.2)$$

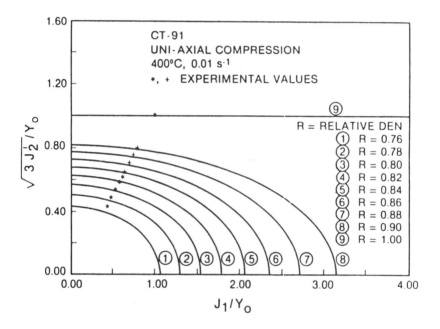

Fig. 3.9 Yield function for various levels of relative-density[9]

Theoretical curves along with experimental results for the uni-axial state of stress are shown in Fig. 3.9 for X7091 aluminium alloy. This figure not only shows good agreement between the theoretical and experimental results but also explains the influence of hydrostatic stress at various density levels. When full densification is achieved, the function automatically becomes the von Mises yield function. Using this yield function, effective stress- and effective strain-relative density relationships have been derived and compared with the experimental results for the uni-axial state of stress

for the same alloy.   Excellent agreement has been observed
between theoretical and experimental results, as shown in Figs.
3.10 and 3.11.

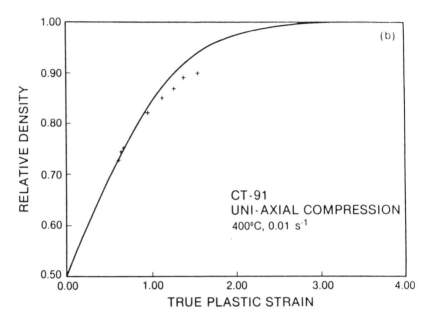

Fig. 3.10 Comparison of theoretical and experimental results[1]

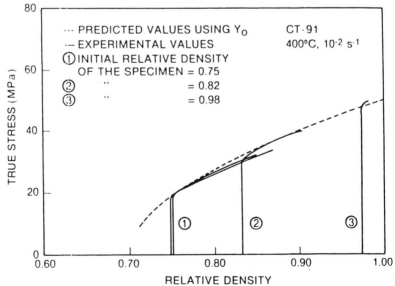

Fig. 3.11 Comparison of theoretical and experimental results[1]

The theory is also applied to various P/M processes such as frictionless closed-die forging, frictionless plane-strain compression, and hydrostatic compression.   These results are presented in Figs. 3.12 and 3.13.

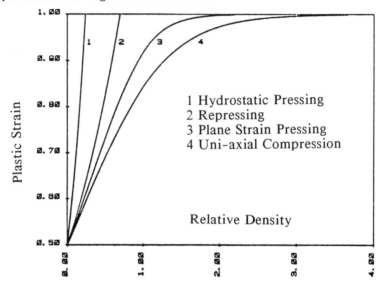

Fig. 3.12 Relative density as a function of plastic strain for various processes[1]

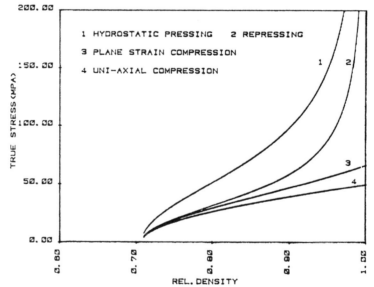

Fig. 3.13 True stress as a function of relative density for various processes[1]

The results show that beyond 95 per cent theoretical density, it is difficult to obtain full densification in hydrostatic and closed-die forging by application of pressure alone, since the pressure required for full densification increases beyond that obtainable by commercial presses. Therefore, this suggests that pressings should be made at a temperature and strain-rate which will accelerate diffusion, to allow full densification to be obtained.

In order to study the effect of strain-rate upon densification during hot working, a constitutive model has been developed by GEGEL et al.[1] for CT 91 (S7091) Al alloy. Uni-axial compression tests have been conducted at different temperatures and strain-rates, as shown in Fig. 3.11, and using these results, the hot-working temperature has been selected. The values of flow stress are plotted in three-dimensional coordinates as a function of density and strain-rate using the computer, as shown in Fig. 3.14. This data base has been used in the model for studying geometric strain hardening (densification) during various metal-forming operations for X7091 ASl-alloy.

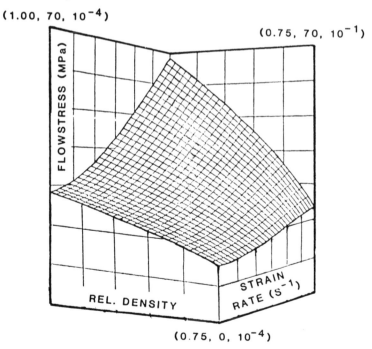

Fig. 3.14 Flow stress as a function of density and strain-rate for CT 91 (S7091) Al alloy powder[1]

3.4.5 *P/M 2024 Al-20 vol% SiC*

A new type of P/M aluminium alloy is being developed which incorporates SiC whiskers into a powder agglomerate for the purpose of increasing the modulus of elasticity and the strength properties of aluminium alloys. These alloys have many attractive properties, but they are difficult to fabricate by metal-working processes. A number of applications exist for these materials in aerospace structural components if they can be extruded or forged into complex geometries without the whiskers fracturing and changing their aspect ratio. The strength properties are strongly dependent upon this ratio, while the effective modulus of elasticity is less strongly influenced by it beyond an aspect ratio of about 12. Figure 3.15 shows the change in aspect ratio of SiC whiskers as a function of processing steps, and Fig. 3.16 shows the dependence of the modulus of elasticity upon the aspect ratio.

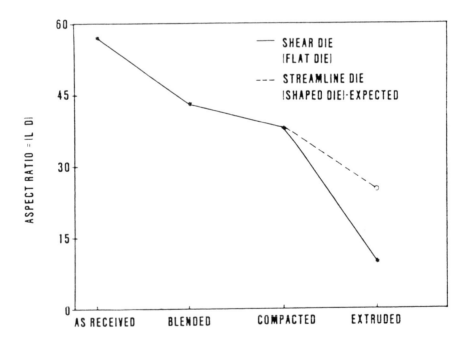

Fig. 3.15 Change in aspect ratio of SiC
whiskers with processing steps[1]

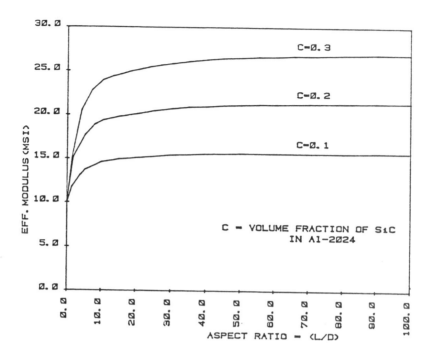

Fig. 3.16 Dependence of elastic modulus
on aspect ratio of SiC whiskers[1]

3.5 Modelling of Dynamic Material Behaviour

The basis for the modelling of dynamic material behaviour is the unifying theme for the modelling of physical systems, as developed by WELLSTEAD[10]; here systems are viewed as energy manipulators. In the metal-processing system, certain elements are stores and sources of energy, while the workpiece is the basic device for dissipating energy. The constitutive equation for the workpiece material is an analytical relation describing the variation of flow stress with process variables, namely, temperature and strain-rate. This equation is an intrinsic characteristic of the workpiece material and describes the manner in which the energy is converted at any instant into a form — usually thermal or microstructural — which is not recoverable by the system. Thus, hot working is modelled in terms of the management of several irreversible thermodynamic processes which are controlled by the rate of energy input and subsequent dissipation of that energy by dynamic metallurgical processes.

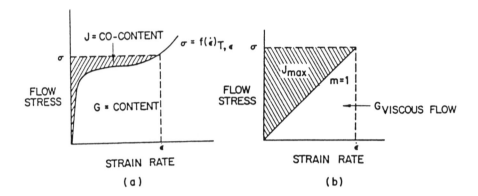

Fig. 3.17 Variation of flow stress with strain-rate[11]

A typical constitutive relation for a simple dissipator is schematically represented in Fig. 3.17 in the form of the variation of flow stress (effort) with strain-rate (flow) at constant temperature and strain. At any given strain-rate, the instantaneous power P absorbed by the workpiece during plastic flow is:-

$$\sigma\dot{\varepsilon} = \int_0^{\dot{\varepsilon}} \sigma d\dot{\varepsilon} + \int_0^{\sigma} \dot{\varepsilon} d\sigma \qquad (3.3a)$$

or:-

$$P = G + J \qquad (3.3b)$$

The G term represents the power dissipated by plastic work, most of which is converted into viscoplastic heat; the little remaining power is stored as lattice defects. The dissipator power co-content J is related to the metallurgical mechanisms which occur dynamically to dissipate power. The G content is the work function in Eq. 3.2, while the J co-content is a complementary set in the variational procedure. The dynamic material behaviour can be modelled explicitly in terms of variations of power co-content J with the process parameters.

3.5.1 Evaluation of Power Co-content J

The constitutive equation which describes the empirical relation between the flow stress and the strain-rate at any temperature can be expressed as:-

$$\dot{\varepsilon} = A\sigma^n \tag{3.4}$$

where A is a constant and n the stress exponent. The term n is related to the strain-rate sensitivity m of the material by:-

$$m = \left[\frac{\Delta \log \sigma}{\Delta \log \dot{\varepsilon}}\right]_T = \frac{1}{n} \tag{3.5}$$

In the hot-working range for pure metals[2], m (or n) is both temperature and strain-rate independent; but in complicated alloy systems, it has been shown[3] to vary with temperature and strain-rate.

At any given deformation temperature, J is evaluated by integrating Eq. 3.4 as follows:-

$$J = \int_0^\sigma \dot{\varepsilon}.d\sigma = A\frac{\sigma^{n+1}}{n+1} \tag{3.6}$$

By combining Eqs. 3.4, 3.5 and 3.6, the J co-content can be related to the strain-rate sensitivity as:-

$$J = \frac{\sigma.\dot{\varepsilon}.m}{m+1} \tag{3.7}$$

In the above integration the strain-rate dependence of m represents the flow trajectory taken by the system to reach the flow stress; according to the variational principle, this is always the path which provides the maximum dissipation co-content J (the "natural" configuration). From Eq. 3.7 the value of J at a given temperature and strain-rate may be estimated from the flow stress and the strain-rate-sensitivity factor m. The value of J reaches its maximum value J_{max} when $m = 1$, and the workpiece acts as a linear dissipator; thus:-

$$J_{max} = \frac{\sigma.\dot{\varepsilon}}{2} \tag{3.8}$$

In this case, one-half of the power is dissipated in material flow and the other half is dissipated in viscous heat (schematically shown in Fig. 3.17). The behaviour of superplastic materials approaches this extreme. The other extreme occurs for materials which are strain-rate insensitive and those which do not flow. In these cases J is zero.

The analogy for the above behaviour is found in certain electrical systems where J_{max} corresponds to good electrical conductors and $J = 0$ corresponds to insulators. Common engineering materials processed at high temperatures exhibit flow behaviour which falls somewhere between these two extremes. These materials are analogous to resistors in electrical systems, and their flow behaviour under dynamic conditions may be characterized in terms of the J co-content. For a given power input to the system, the material flow will be maximum when the workpiece dissipates the highest poss-ible power through dynamic metallurgical processes, i.e., the J co-content reaches its highest value.

The effect of J on the plastic flow of materials can be visualized if the power-dissipation capacity of the workpiece is expressed in terms of an efficiency of dissipation, η, which is defined as the ratio of J to J_{max}. From Equations 3.7 and 3.8, it follows that:-

$$\eta = \frac{J}{J_{max}} = \frac{2m}{m+1} \qquad (3.9)$$

In simple terms the efficiency represents the dissipating ability of the workpiece as normalized with respect to the total power input to the system.

Several dynamic metallurgical processes contribute to power dissipation during hot working of materials, and these processes have characteristic ranges of efficiencies of dissipation. In materials having complicated microstructures or in two-phase alloys, these processes often occur simultaneously and/or interactively. Thus, the evaluated value of J will be the overall result of these interactions. Metallurgical processes such as dynamic recovery, dynamic recrystallization, internal fracture (void formation or wedge cracking), dissolution or growth of particles or phases under dynamic conditions, dyn-amic spheroidization of acicular structures, and deformation-induced phase transformation or precipitation under dynamic conditions contribute to the changes in the dissipated power co-content J. When two major dissipation processes having different characteristics occur simultaneously, the value of J will reach its maximum when the energy of dissipation of one process equals that of the other. This is somewhat analogous to what happens in electrical systems having a variable resistor where the load power reaches a maximum when the line and load resistance are equal. For processing of materials the most favourable conditions are those which provide the highest J dissipated in the most efficient fashion (highest η) and which lie within the "safe" regions.

The power co-content J serves as the most useful index

for characterizing dynamic material behaviour in processing, for the following reasons:-

1.   It defines unique combinations of T and $\dot\varepsilon$ for processing (peak values of J and η) and also separates the régimes which produce internal fracture.

2.   Being a power term, it is an invariant and, hence, applicable to any state of stress.

3.   It can be used conveniently as a non-holonomic constraint in the finite element method.

4.   It is a continuum parameter and can be integrated with the finite element analysis.

5.   In its estimation, no specific atomistic rate-controlling mechanisms need to be evaluated or assumed, although its variation with temperature and strain-rate reflects the dominating dissipating mechanism. This aspect is advantageous, particularly when more than one mechanism is operating during hot forming.

3.5.2 Material Stability[12]

To establish proper stability criteria for metal forming applications, Liapunov functions have been formulated in terms of the process variables. The Liapunov function is a quantity associated with the Liapunov function stability criteria which is one of the most accepted methods in engineering design.[13]
A new coefficient s has been defined by GEGEL[14] and associates. s is the temperature sensitivity of stress.

$$s = \frac{1}{T} \frac{\delta(\log\sigma)}{\delta(1/T)} \bigg|_{\epsilon,\dot\varepsilon} \qquad (3.10)$$

Two conditions are used in the dynamic modelling approach for stability criteria:

$$\frac{\delta m}{\delta(\log\dot\varepsilon)} < 0 \quad ; \quad \frac{\delta s}{\delta(\log\dot\varepsilon)} < 0 \qquad (3.11)$$

These two conditions are used in the development of processing maps. Several dynamic models have been developed by GOPINATH[15] to illustrate the validity of this analysis.

3.5.3 *Data Analysis by MIS (Material Information System)*[15]

MIS is an extremely userfriendly and interactive program which has been developed by Gopinath and Gunasekera and later refined by UES (Universal Energy System) Inc., Dayton, Ohio, USA, to perform the task of dynamic material behaviour modelling. It is not necessary for the user to have extensive knowledge of computers and/or dynamic material behaviour modelling in order to use this package. Typical results obtained using MIS on AL-5Si alloy at 0.6 strain are given in Fig. 3.18 and Fig. 3.19.

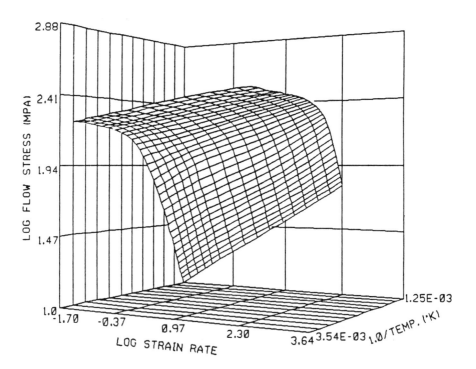

Fig. 3.18 Three dimensional plot of log flow stress of Al-5Si alloy at 0.6 strain[15]

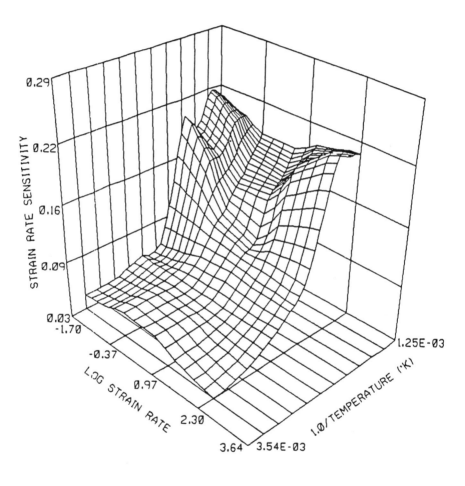

Fig. 3.19 Three dimensional plot of strain rate sensitivity of
Al-5Si alloy at 0.6 strain[15]

Fig. 3.20 shows the stability map for the Al-5Si alloy. The shaded region satisfies the criteria in equation 3.11, and indicates the stable regions for processing without generating any defects.

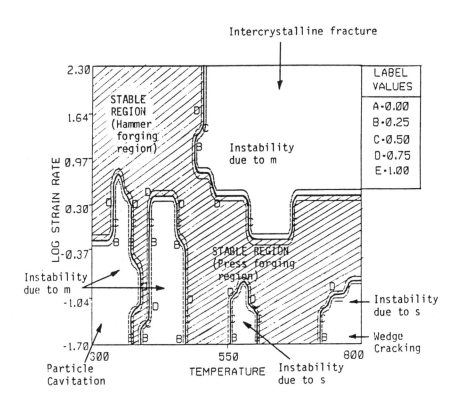

Fig. 3.20 Stability map showing safe processing regions for Al-5Si alloy at 0.6 strain[15]

REFERENCES

(1) GEGEL, H.L., GUNASEKERA, J.S., DORAIVELU, S.M., MALAS, J.C., MORGAN, J.T. and MATSON, L.E., "Consolidation and Forming of P/M Porous Billets" *Presented at the 3rd Conference on Rapid Solidification Process*, Gaithersburgh, MD, USA., Dec 6-8, 1982.

(2) HILDEMAN, G.J., LEGE, D.J. and VASUDEVAN, A.K., *Fundamentals of Compaction Processes for Rapidly Quenched Prealloyed Metal Powders*. Technical Report. Alcoa Technical Center, Pennsylvania, 1982.

(3) ZHDANOVICH, G.M., "Theory of Compacting Metal Powders", *Teorize Pressovaniye Metzillchaskikli Poroshkov* 1969, pp. 1-262 (U.S.A.F. Translation FTD-HCC-23-775-70).

(4) KUHN, H.A., "Deformation Processing of Sintered Powder Metals", Chap. 4 in *Powder Metallurgy Processing: New Techniques and Analysis*. Academic Press, New York, 1978.

(5) GREEN, R.J.,"A Plasticity Theory for Porous Solids" *Int. J. Mech. Sci.* 1972, **14**, 215.

(6) OYANE, M., SHIMA, S. and KONO, Y, "Theory of Plasticity for Porous Metals", *Bull. J.S.M.E.* 1973, **16**, 1254.

(7) SHIMA, S. and OYANE, M., "Plasticity Theory for Porpous Metals", *Int. J. Mech. Sci.* 1976, **18**, 285.

(8) KUHN, H.A. and DOWNEY, C.L., "Material Behavior in Powder Preform Forging" *J. Eng. Mat. Tech.* 1973, pp. 41

(9) DORAIVELU, S.M., GEGEL, H.L., MALAS, J.C., GUNASEKRA, J.S., and THOMAS, J.F., "A New Yield Function for Compressible P/M Materials", Int. J. of Mech. Sci., 1984, 26(9/10), 527-535.

(10) WELLSTEAD, P.E., "*Introduction to Physical Modeling*", Academic Press, New York, 1979, pp. 9-144.

(11) PRASAD, Y.V.R.K., GEGEL, H.L., DORAIVELU, S.M., MALAS, J.C., MORGAN, J.T., LARK, K.A., and BARKER, D.R., "Modeling of Dynamic Material Behavior in Hot Deformation; Forging Ti 6242", *Metall. Trans.*, 1984, A 15, 1883.

(12) MALAS, J.C., "A Thermodynamic and Continuum Approach to the Design and Control of Precision Forging Processes", *Master's Thesis*, Wright State University, 1985.

(13) SCHULTZ, D.G., and MELSA, J.L., "State Functions and Linear Control Systems", McGraw Hill, 1967, pp. 155-195.

(14) GEGEL, H.L., MALAS, J.C., DORAIVELU, S.M., ALEXANDER, J.M., and GUNASEKERA, J.S., "Materials Modeling and Intrinsic Workability", *Trans. Int. Conf. Tech. of Plasticity*, Stuttgart, Aug. 1987.

(15) GOPINATH, S., "Automation of the Data Analysis System used in Process Modeling Appilcations", *Master's Thesis*, Ohio University, 1986.

Chapter 4

COMPUTER GRAPHICS FOR DIE DESIGN AND MANUFACTURE

4.1 Introduction

Computer graphics involves the creation and manipulation of pictures with the aid of a computer. Such pictures may be generated either on a graphics terminal or on paper using a computer-controlled plotter, and are referred to as non-interactive or passive computer graphics. The observer or user has no control over the image. When the user is given some control over the image by providing him with a user device such as a joystick, it is termed interactive computer graphics. Hence interactive computer graphics involve a two-way communication between the computer and the user.

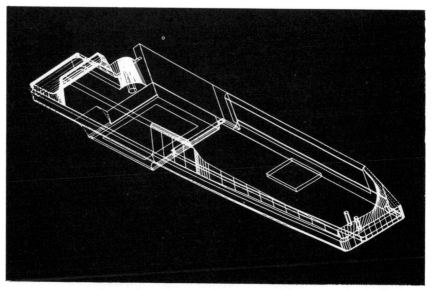

Fig. 4.1 Computer-generated line drawing
(Courtesy of Intergraph Corp.)

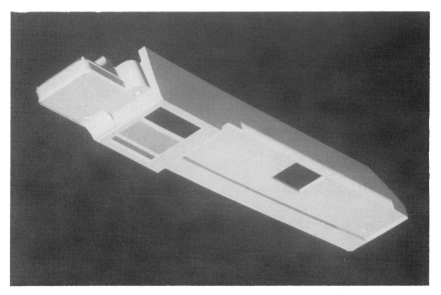

Fig. 4.2 Computer-generated continuous-tone image
(Courtesy of Intergraph Corp.)

The main advantage of the use of interactive computer graphics in die design and manufacture is the user's ability to interact with the computer quickly to correct a design error and/or to optimize the design by interactively modifying the design with the help of the computer.

Computer-generated pictures may be divided broadly into two classes:- line drawings and continuous-tone images. Examples of each are shown in Figs. 4.1 and 4.2. These two classes of picture differ in appearance and are also generated using different techniques. Line drawings are in general easier to create because the algorithms for their generation are simpler and the amount of information required for their presentation is less.

4.2 Display Devices and Controller

The display device converts electrical signals into visible images. The display controller sits between the computer and the display device, receiving information from the computer and converting it into signals acceptable to the device. The display controller converts the voltage-level between the computer and the display device, buffers to compensate for differences in speed of operation and generates various forms of line segments and text characters. Some display controllers are designed with additional hardware to perform graphic functions such as scaling, rotation, zooming, etc., that would otherwise be performed by software in the host computer. In general this procedure improves the response speed because of the local in-built intelligence.

There is a large variety of display devices. The following is a list of some of the more common types:-

   (a)   CRT (Cathode Ray Tube)
   (b)   DVST (Direct-View Storage Tube)
   (c)   Plasma panel
   (d)   Laser-scan display
   (e)   Storage-tube display
   (f)   Refresh line-drawing display
   (g)   Raster-scan display

A typical graphics terminal (Tektronix 4200 series) is shown in Fig. 4.3. It incorporates a raster scan display, a built-in alphanumeric keyboard, and an optional mouse. The screen coordinate system is divided into 640 positions horizontally and 480 positions vertically. The display can be used both as an alphanumeric text terminal and as a graphics display.

The refresh line-drawing display is very similar to the storage-tube display except that the controller operates at high speed to maintain a flicker-free picture by feeding a fresh description of the picture 30 or so times a second. For this purpose it makes use of a display process that can function entirely independently of the CPU.

The disadvantges of the CRT were the flicker when displaying complex objects and also it could not produce realistic images of solid objects. The raster display promised to solve both problems. The only limitation of the raster display was the poor resolution which has been improved dramatically with advances in raster technology.

The raster display devices fall into two distinct classes; video devices and matrix-address storage devices. They are similar in the sense that they both use a rectangular array of pixels to generate images. The main difference between the two kinds of display lies in the absence of image storage in video displays and its presence in matrix displays. The TV monitor is the most common video device. Since there is no image-storage capacity, the display image must be passed repeatedly to the device, at a high enough speed (refresh rate) to prevent flicker. In the matrix-addressed storage display of which the plasma panel is the best known, the screen is divided into a matrix of cells, each one of which can be individually turned on or off to produce the desired image. This requires only a simple controller that turns cells on or off in response to signals from the computer.

Most raster-scan displays use video-display devices based on the use of a large digital memory or frame buffer, to store the displayed image. Many different kinds of memory have been used in frame buffers; drums, disks, integrated circuit registers, and core stores. Nowadays most frame buffers are constructed from random-access integrated-circuit memories. Each pixel's intensity is represented by 1, 2, 4, 8, or more bits of memory. One bit is sufficient for text and simple graphics and leads to a relatively inexpensive display. Two and four bits are useful in applications that require the display of solid areas of grey, or colour; eight or more bits are needed for high-quality shaded pictures.

4.3 Three-dimensional Graphics

Computer graphics applications in the CAD/CAM of dies involve the display of 2- and 3-dimensional objects. For example, the user can interactively design a die and then display it on the screen. The user may rotate or zoom it up to understand better the 3-D geometry of the die. Finally, the user may wish to see the object in perspective with hidden lines removed or in colour with shading. Images used in die design and manufacture now offer enough realism for the user to evaluate the design — in terms of its general application as well as satisfying the various criteria for optimum design and 'manufacturability'.

4.4 Curves and Surfaces

Special techniques have to be developed in order to represent realistic images of complex 3-D geometries of dies. The geometry of a die may be approximated to a collection of plane-faced polyhedra with straight edges. However, such a representation may involve hundreds or thousands of faces and edges and would clearly be cumbersome to generate and to modify. Hence it is necessary to represent the surface of the die as a collection of curved sculptured surface patches bounded by curved edges. Irrespective of the method used to represent complex surfaces the geometry has to be modelled in a mathematical form suitable for a computer.

The modelling system must support a class of shapes that is matched to the design applications. To design a majority of mechanical parts, shapes limited to plane faced polyhedra and sections of cylinders may be adequate. On the other hand to design a complex shape such as a die (or an automobile or aircraft body) a more versatile and flexible system of shapes and techniques to maintain the smoothness of the shape is needed.

The design process is very often iterative. The designer will carefully observe the shape designed and check whether the design is acceptable (or optimal) based on various criteria and develop ideas to change it. The software and the hardware of the system must therefore permit such interaction between the designer and the computer and be fully interactive and user-friendly, for maximum productivity. It is also important that the scheme used for modelling curves and surfaces should be capable of mathematical representation, computationally convenient and economical of storage. The following is a number of properties that the scheme should have. These requirements are for a curve, and surfaces can be represented using simple extensions of the techniques used for representing curves.

(i)   Control points − may be on the curve or outside on a polygon (Fig. 4.4).

(ii)   Multiple values − a curve may have multiple values (Fig. 4.5).

(iii)   Axis independence − the shape of the die should be independent of the axis chosen (Fig. 4.6).

(iv)   Global or local control − a fine local adjustment to a die should not affect the rest of the geometry (Fig. 4.7).

(v)   Variation-diminishing property − smoothness (Fig. 4.8).

(vi)   Versatility − curves should be versatile.

(vii)   Order of continuity − the designer may want to join pieces of curves with order of continuity control of the points. Zero-order continuity means that the curves meet. First-order continuity requires the curves to be tangent at the point of intersection. Second-order continuity requires that curvature be the same (Fig. 4.9).

Fig. 4.3 Tektronix 4200 series display
(Courtesy of Tektronix Corp.)

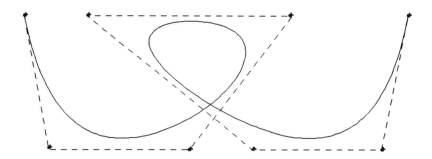

Fig. 4.4 Control points

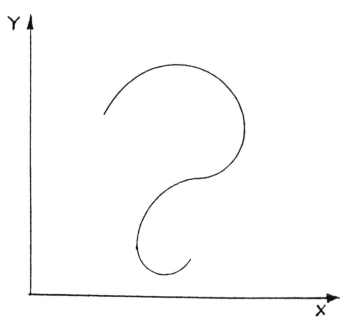

Fig. 4.5 Multiple values

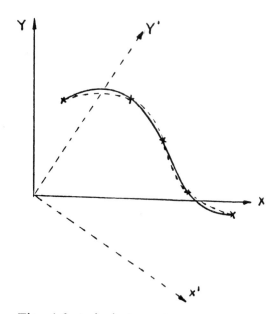

Fig. 4.6 Axis independence

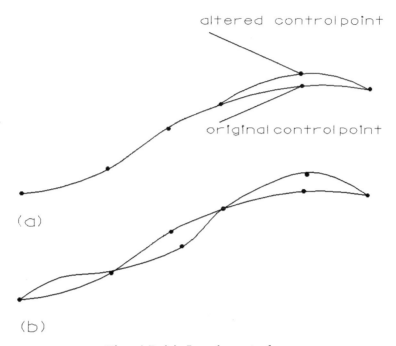

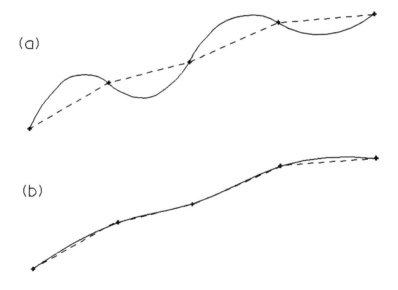

Fig. 4.7 (a) Local control.
(b) Global control

Fig. 4.8 (a) Oscillating curve.
(b) Variation-diminishing curve

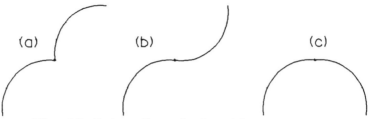

Fig. 4.9 Order of continuity: (a) zero-order,
(b) first-order, (c) second-order

The above requirements have led to the use of 'parametric' or
'vector-valued' methods for the representation of curves and
surfaces: thus instead of forcing all curves to be of the form:-

$$y = f(x) \qquad (4.1)$$

and surfaces of the form:-

$$z = f(x,y) \qquad (4.2)$$

we can employ 'vector-valued' or 'parametric' functions.
For plane curves:-

$$\underline{P}(u) = [x(u)\ y(u)] \qquad (4.3)$$

and for surfaces:-

$$\underline{P}(u,v) = [x(u,v)\ y(u,v)\ z(u,v)] \qquad (4.4)$$

where $\underline{P}$ is a point vector.
An important feature of any computer-aided design
system handling geometry and shape information is its ability
to bound curves and surfaces. The classical mathematics of
surfaces rarely occurs in its entirety in most engineering
applications. Any shape representation must allow the user to
specify the boundaries of the shape in a simple manner. The
vector-valued method allows bounding very elegantly by
merely specifying the range of the parametric variables. (In
classical surface geometry, bounding would be far more
complex.)
In the case of curves, the bounds would be:-

$u = 0$ and $u = 1$,

whereas $0 < u < 1$ denotes the curve segment of interest.
In the case of surfaces, the bounds are:-

$u = 0,\ u = 1,\ v = 0,\ v = 1$

4.4.1 *Coons' Surfaces*

Computer-aided design of objects is not solely concerned with pictorial properties of shape but with providing a geometric model or geometric data base which can then be used for design, analysis and manufacture (i.e. production of NC tape etc.). This problem was tackled by Professor Coons at M.I.T. in the early sixties (1964, actually) (COONS[1]). Coons' methods were very quickly adopted by industry – in the design and manufacture of aircraft exterior parts, ship hulls and automobile bodies. Coons used two important concepts (mentioned before) namely (i) parametric representation and (ii) piecewise or patch representation. (Another researcher, FERGUSON[2] of the Boeing Company, published the same concept at about the same time - however, the surfaces are widely referred to as "Coons' Surfaces").

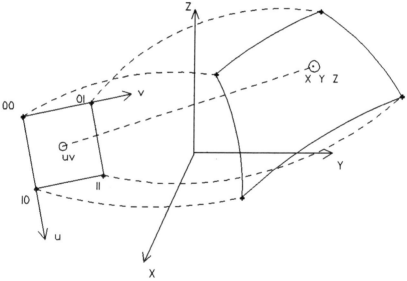

Fig. 4.10 Bi-cubic patch

The surface to be designed would then consist of an assembly of surface patches or elements (each patch being defined analytically) and interconnected at their edges with a given boundary condition. The common bi-cubic patch satisfies slope continuity at the edges in addition to positional continuity (Fig. 4.10). The bi-cubic surface patch is of particular interest in the present case and will be dealt with in some detail. Coons' methods build up surfaces from known data (i.e. at the boundaries); and we shall denote the known data by P and resulting surface by Q. P and Q will coincide at the specified boundary points.

The derivative of the vectors can be denoted as:-

$$\underline{P}^{a,b}(u,v) = \frac{\partial^{a+b}\,\underline{P}(u,v)}{\partial u^a \partial v^b}$$

and the scalar blending functions as:-

$$\beta_{r,i}(u) \text{ and } \beta_{s,j}(v)$$

The problem of constructing a bi-cubic patch may be viewed mathematically as a problem of mapping a unit square in the parameter $(u\text{-}v)$ plane into a surface in the (x,y,z) three-dimensional space.

The bi-cubic patch takes the form:-

$$Q(u,v) = \sum_{i=0}^{i=1}\sum_{j=0}^{j=1}\sum_{r=0}^{r=1}\sum_{s=0}^{s=1} \underline{P}^{r,s}{}_{i,j}\,\beta_{r,i}(u)\,\beta_{s,j}(v) \quad (4.7)$$

where:-
$$\beta_{0,0}(u) = 1-3u^2+2u^3$$

$$\beta_{0,1}(u) = 3u^2-2u^3$$

$$\beta_{1,0}(v) = v-2v^2+v^3 \quad (4.8)$$

$$\beta_{1,1}(u) = -v^2+v^3$$

or:-
$$Q(u,v) = [\,u^3\ u^2\ u^1\,]\underline{M}\ \underline{B}\ \underline{M}^t[\,v^3\ v^2\ v^1\,]^t \quad (4.9)$$

where:-
$$\underline{M} = \begin{bmatrix} 2 & -2 & 1 & 1 \\ -3 & 3 & -2 & -1 \\ 0 & 0 & 1 & 0 \\ 1 & 0 & 0 & 0 \end{bmatrix}$$

is a 4×4 matrix, and:-

$$\underline{B} = \begin{bmatrix} \underline{P}(0,0) & \underline{P}(0,1) & \underline{P}^{0,1}(0,0) & \underline{P}^{0,1}(0,1) \\ \underline{P}(1,0) & \underline{P}(1,1) & \underline{P}^{0,1}(1,0) & \underline{P}^{0,1}(1,1) \\ \underline{P}^{1,0}(0,0) & \underline{P}^{1,0}(0,1) & \underline{P}^{1,1}(0,0) & \underline{P}^{1,1}(0,1) \\ \underline{P}^{1,0}(1,0) & \underline{P}^{1,0}(1,1) & \underline{P}^{1,1}(1,0) & \underline{P}^{1,1}(1,1) \end{bmatrix} \quad (4.10)$$

is a tensor:-

where $\underline{P}_{(i,j)}$ is the point vector.

$$\underline{P}^{1,0}(i,j) = \frac{\partial \underline{P}(i,j)}{\partial u} \quad \text{is the tangent vector in the } u \text{ direction}$$

$$\underline{P}^{0,1}(i,j) = \frac{\partial \underline{P}(i,j)}{\partial v} \quad \text{is the tangent vector in the } v \text{ direction}$$

$$\underline{P}^{1,0}(i,j) = \frac{\partial^2 \underline{P}(i,j)}{\partial u \ \partial v} \quad \text{is the twist vector at } i,j$$

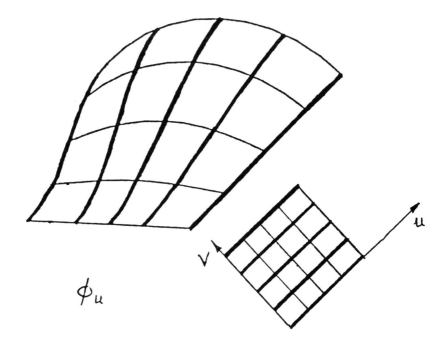

Fig. 4.11 Lofting method

The bi-cubic surface patch is convenient in that the slope continuity of adjacent patches at the edges can be maintained (in addition to the positional continuity). However it is not easy practice for a designer to specify tangent vectors - both in magnitude and direction; and the twist vectors (having no immediate physical meaning) are much more difficult to define. The problem can be overcome by other methods such as "Lofting" (GORDON[3]) and Bézier's method (BÉZIER[4,5]).

The surface in this case is defined in terms of a number of curves (see Fig. 4.11). The curves themselves might be obtained by a spline technique (using a number of points). By defining the surface in terms of a spline blend of curves, greater flexibility is obtained as compared with the previous procedure.

Lofting can be generalized as:-

$$Q(u,v) = \sum_{i=0}^{i=M} \sum_{r=0}^{r=m_i} \underline{P}^{r,0}(u_i,v)\beta_{r,i}(u) \qquad (4.11)$$

$$Q(u,v) = \sum_{j=0}^{j=N} \sum_{s=0}^{s=n_i} \underline{P}^{0,s}(u,v_j)\beta_{r,i}(v) \qquad (4.11)$$

The procedure used in die design is essentially a Lofting technique. This technique is also widely used in the aerospace industry and in ship design. In the former case the sections may be either cross-sections across the fuselage or sections down the fuselage. In the latter case, waterlines or bulkheads are the prime design variables in defining a hull.

The surface is essentially defined by one family of functions – say functions of constant u, and a check can be made on the other family of functions of constant v. The process can be iterated to refine the surface. Lofting uses not only the grid intersection data, but also one set of grid lines – and this leads to extra control over the surface. However, this added control may be biased towards one particular parametric direction.

In the design of shaped extrusion dies (or propulsive nozzles) the extra control along a particular direction is used to an advantage by defining the family of functions in the direction of extrusion (or flow of gas) – i.e. along the axial direction. This procedure ensures smooth flow of metal (or gas) through the die (or the nozzle) which is primarily in the axial direction.

Some of the well known systems based on Lofting are the Autokon system, Oslo, Norway (BATES[6]), the Numerical Master Geometry system at the British Aircraft Corporation, Warton and the Loft system at McDonnell-Douglas, St. Louis.

4.4.2 Bézier Method

A Frenchman, P. Bézier, developed a system known as UNISURF for generating curved surfaces. These can be used for describing the surfaces of automobiles or dies. However, it should be noted that the curve or surface does not pass through all of the points. Instead it passes only through the first and last point. The other points should not be specified as points on the surface but rather as control points that pull or tease the curve or surface in its direction.

Of the desired properties, the Bézier curve has all but one. The Bézier curve has global control, not local. This means that if a control point is changed then the complete die surface will change.

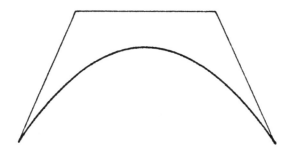

Fig. 4.12 Example Bézier curve

The Bézier equation is a function of u. The value u is the distance along the curve. The value of u is 0.0 at the beginning point and is 1.0 at the end of the curve. The basic form of the Bézier curve is:-

$$P(u) = \sum_{i=0}^{i=n} p_i \, B_{i,n}(u)$$

p_i is the value of the i control point and $B_{i,n}(u)$ is the blending function:-

$$B_{i,n}(u) = C(n,i)u^i(1-u)^{n-i}$$

where:-

$$C(n,i) = n!/\{i!(n-i)!\}.$$

is the binomial coefficient.

Fig. 4.12 shows an example Bézier curve in the plane; the z coordinate of each control point is zero. The particular curve shown used four control points, connected in the illustration to form an open "polygon."

The blending functions are the key to the behaviour of Bézier curves. Fig. 4.13 shows the four blending functions that correspond to a Bézier curve with four control points. These curves represent the "influence" that each control point exerts on the curve for various values of u. The first control point, p_0, corresponding to $B_{0,3}(u)$, is most influential when

$u=0$; in fact, locations of all other control points are ignored when $u=0$, because their blending functions are zero. The situation is symmetric for P_3 and $u=1$. The middle control points P_1 and P_2 are most influential when $u = 1/3$ and $2/3$, respectively.

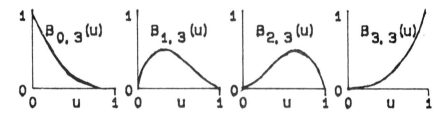

Fig. 4.13 The four blending functions

The main features of Bézier curves may be summarized as follows:-

1. Control points. At first, it might seem that Bézier curves are hard to use because not all control points lie on the curve. However, the curve is predictably related to the locations of control points — each seems to exert a "pull" on the portion of the curve near it. The control points also satisfy two important mathematical properties: the curve does pass through the two endpoints (P_0 and P_n), and the curve is tangent at the endpoints to the corresponding edge of the polygon of control points (e.g., the curve at $P\_$is tangent to the vector joining P_0 and P_1).

2. Multiple values. The parametric formulation of the Bézier curve allows it to represent multiple-valued shapes. In fact, if the first and last control points coincide, the curve is closed.

3. Axis independence. A Bézier curve is independent of the coordinate system used to measure the locations of control points.

4. Global or local control. These curves do not provide localized control: moving any control point will change the shape of every part of the curve.

5. Variation-diminishing property. It may be seen that Bézier curves are variation-diminishing. In addition a curve is guaranteed to lie within the convex hull of the control points that define it (GORDON and RIESENFELD[7]). Thus the Bézier curve never oscillates wildly away from its defining control points.

6. Versatility. The versatility of a Bézier curve is governed by the number of control points used. In the example of Fig. 4.12, four control points are used ($n=3$) to determine two parametric cubic polynomial functions that specify x and y values. More control points can always be used to describe more complex shapes, but eventually the high-order polynomial equations become difficult to use because of the lack of localized control.

7. Order of continuity. Bézier curves of modest order can be pieced together to describe a more complex curve. In these cases, the points between the curves must be smooth.[8]

For the purpose of a graphic display of the die the surface form of the Bézier curve is more useful. The surface form is the Cartesian product of two curves. This means that P is a function of u and v and takes the form:-

$$P(u,v) = \sum_{i=0}^{i=n} \sum_{j=0}^{j=m} P_{i,j} \, B_{i,n}(u) \, B_{j,m}(v)$$

The result of this equation is a surface that has constant u lines and constant v lines (see Fig. 3.3). The control points for a Bézier curve are set up in a mesh formation. It is still true that the surface does not pass through all the control points.

This can be seen in Fig. 4.14 which shows just half of the die. In order to make a continuous connection of the edge BC with the other corresponding edge on the other half, two things must be done. First, all of the control points of the mesh between point B and point C must be the same control points specified on the corresponding edge of the opposite mesh. Second, all line segments like AB and DE must have the same slope as their corresponding line segments on the opposite mesh.

Because there is no local control, the best method of assuring symmetry on both halves of the dies is to make the two meshes exact opposites and a slope of zero in segments like AB.

Complete closed loops or closed curves, such as cylinders, can also be made with Bézier equations. This can be done by specifying the beginning and end points as the same values.

In order to achieve the effect of local control in a long curve or surface when using Bézier equations, many smaller parts are pieced together. A change in one control point would affect only its corresponding section.

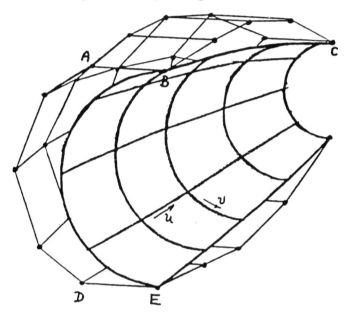

Fig. 4.14 Half of a die surface as
created by a Bézier equation

4.4.3 *B-spline Method*

As has been shown, there are some drawbacks to the Bézier curves. The B-spline can solve some of these problems. With the use of the B-spline one can control the shape of the die surface much better. But it is harder to calculate the blending function $\{N_{i,k}(u)\}$.

The B-spline has the same general form as the Bézier curve, but u has a range from 0.0 to $n-k+2$. The k value which is used in the calculation of $N_{i,k}(u)$ controls the order of continuity of the curve. The smaller is the k value, the closer will the spline follow the contour of the mesh. The equation for determining the blending function is:-

$$N_{i,1}(u) = 1 \quad \text{if } t_i \leqslant u < t_{i+1}, \text{ or}$$
$$N_{i,1}(u) = 0 \quad \text{otherwise.}$$

Because the denominator can go to zero the convention is used to accept 0.0/0.0 as 0.0. The equation for $N_{i,k}(u)$ is:-

$$N_{i,k}(u) = \frac{(u-t_i)N_{i,k-1}(u)}{t_{i+k-1} - t_i} + \frac{(t_{i+k}-u)N_{i+1,k-1}(u)}{t_{i+k} - t_{i+1}}$$

The above equation for $N_{i,k}(u)$ contains t_i which is known as a knot value which depends on whether the spline is open or closed and on the relation of i to k and n.

For an open loop the following rules can be used:-

(1) if $i < k$ then $t_i = 0$
(2) if $k <$ or $= i <$ or $= n$ then $t_i = i-k+1$
(3) if $i > n$ then $t_i = n-k+2$

The best way to generate the blending function for the closed spline is to let $t_i = i$.

The surface form of the B-spline has the general form:-

$$P(u,v) = \sum_{i=0}^{i=n} \sum_{j=0}^{j=m} P_{i,j}\, N_{i,k}(u)\, N_{j,l}(v)$$

This is the same Cartesian product method used by the Bézier curve.

The B-spline has many advantages over the Bézier curve. The B-spline has the same advantages of being able to handle multivalued curves, axis independence, and it does not amplify small irregularities.   But the B-spline has local control and requires less piecing together of the spline.   In fact, the B-spline can produce a sharp corner without piecing two splines together as must be done with the Bézier curves.   This is accomplished by designating three or more control points with the same X,Y,Z value.

4.5 Data Transformations[8]

Once the graphic display of the die is completed, it is often desired to manipulate the die on the screen.   In order to accomplish this one must have the capability to rotate, to move to either side or up and down, and to remove hidden lines from the graphic display of the die.

4.5.1 Rotation

So that the observer has the ability to look at the die from all sides one must have the capability to rotate the image about all three axes.   In the following transformation equations the point (X,Y,Z) is transformed to the values

(X',Y',Z'). The resulting direction of rotation of the following three matrices can be seen in Fig. 4.15.

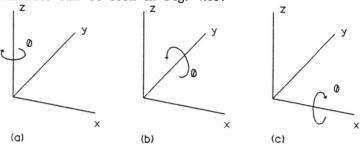

Fig. 4.15 Directions of rotation

The following transformations are used:-

(i)   for the rotation about the Z axis:-

$$[X',Y',Z',1.0] = [X,Y,Z,1.0] \begin{bmatrix} \cos\theta & -\sin\theta & 0.0 & 0.0 \\ \sin\theta & \cos\theta & 0.0 & 0.0 \\ 0.0 & 0.0 & 1.0 & 0.0 \\ 0.0 & 0.0 & 0.0 & 1.0 \end{bmatrix}$$

(ii) for the rotation about the Y axis:-

$$[X',Y',Z',1.0] = [X,Y,Z,1.0] \begin{bmatrix} \cos\theta & 0.0 & \sin\theta & 0.0 \\ 0.0 & 1.0 & 0.0 & 0.0 \\ \sin\theta & 0.0 & \cos\theta & 0.0 \\ 0.0 & 0.0 & 0.0 & 1.0 \end{bmatrix}$$

(iii) for the rotation about the X axis:-

$$[X',Y',Z',1.0] = [X,Y,Z,1.0] \begin{bmatrix} 1.0 & 0.0 & 0.0 & 0.0 \\ 0.0 & \cos\theta & -\sin\theta & 0.0 \\ 0.0 & \sin\theta & \cos\theta & 0.0 \\ 0.0 & 0.0 & 0.0 & 1.0 \end{bmatrix}$$

4.5.2 *Scaling*

If it is necessary to scale the graphic display of the die up or down in size, another matrix transformation can be used. The scaling value is denoted by S. This value is broken into X, Y and Z values. It is best to have the scaling values of all components equal so that the image is not distorted. The transformation matrix for scaling is:-

$$[X',Y',Z',1.0] = [X,Y,Z,1.0] \begin{bmatrix} Sx & 0.0 & 0.0 & 0.0 \\ 0.0 & Sy & 0.0 & 0.0 \\ 0.0 & 0.0 & Sz & 0.0 \\ 0.0 & 0.0 & 0.0 & 1.0 \end{bmatrix}$$

4.5.3 *Translation*

The translation of the die can be accomplished by adding the distance it is wished to move the die to the X, Y, or Z value depending on which direction one wishes to move the die. The matrix form of this addition is:-

$$[X',Y',Z',1.0] = [X,Y,Z,1.0] \begin{bmatrix} 1.0 & 0.0 & 0.0 & 0.0 \\ 0.0 & 1.0 & 0.0 & 0.0 \\ 0.0 & 0.0 & 1.0 & 0.0 \\ Tx & Ty & Tz & 1.0 \end{bmatrix}$$

4.5.4 *Hidden Line Removal*

The transformations just discussed are quite simple. In all three transformations the operation could be performed on all of the data with just one function. This is not true for the task of removing hidden lines.

The operation of removing hidden lines or surfaces must be handled differently depending on the graphic display method. If raster scan is being used then a simple method of determining the pixel depth is used. If raster scan is not being used then the method of geometric relations is used. This is a lengthy process that requires many steps.

As discussed before, the raster scan method creates surfaces that are filled in to give the appearance of being solid. This is done by turning all the pixels within the defined area. Associated with each pixel is an X and Y value that determines the position of the pixel. For each X and Y value there could be many Z values, each having a different intensity. The question becomes; which intensity of light should this pixel represent since the die surface should represent a solid piece of metal: the intensity of light associated with the smallest Z value should be represented by the pixel. The idea is simple; however it is a lengthy process that requires a large amount of memory space.

There are many methods for hidden line removal using the geometric relationships. For representing the die with the wire frame method, special criteria must be met in order to give a good graphics display of the die without the hidden lines.

All of the methods apply three basic tests. They are a visibility test, a relationship test and a depth test. The order in which the tests are applied could vary according to the specific method.

The following method was designed to be for the die designing package called STREAM. This is a very simple-to-use package that creates stream-lined die designs.

The first test that will be performed is the depth test. The die is divided into quadrilaterals. The sides are made of straight lines that are defined by two points. The computer is first asked to take each element and determine which of the points in the die are covered by another surface. Each point that is covered by another surface is marked with a one, while those that are not covered will be preformed. This test checks to see which of the elements are totally covered. This is done simply by checking if all of the four vertices are flagged as one. If so, the complete element is covered and it is therefore removed from the memory. This leaves only the elements that are partly or totally exposed.

Now the final test is applied. This is the relationship test. Here the computer must determine at what point on the sides of the element does the element become covered. One can check this by using only a two-dimensional view of the graphic display (use only X and Y components of each point). The point of intersection is then found between the two lines that represent the edge of the element that is half covered and the edge of the element that is covering. This is done for all sides that have a point flagged by one and the other flagged as zero. If both end points are flagged as one, the connectivity is dropped between the two points. Now that the point of intersection is determined the end point that was flagged as one is redefined as this point of intersection. After this is done for all half covered elements then all hidden lines have been removed.

REFERENCES

(1) COONS, S.A., "Surfaces for Computer-Aided Design of Space Figures", *ESL 9442-M-139 M.I.T.*, 1969.

(2) FERGUSON, J., "Multivariable Curve Interpolation", *J. Assoc. for Computing Machinery* 1964, 11(2), 221-228.

(3) GORDON,W.J., "Blending function methods of bivariate and multivariate interpolation and approximation", *SIAM J. Numer. Anal.* 1971, 8(1).

(4) BÉZIER, P.E., "Example of an existing system in the motor industry: The Unisurf system", *Proc. Roy. Soc. Lond.* 1971, A.321, 207-218.

(5) BÉZIER, P.E., *Numerical Control – Mathematics and Applications.* John Wiley, London, 1972.

(6) BATES, K.J., "The AUTOKON automotive and aerospace packages", *Curved Surfaces in Engineering.* IPC Press, 1972, 19-22.

(7) GORDON, W.J. and RIESENFELD, R.F., "Bernstein-Bezier Methods for the Computer-Aided-Design of Free-Form Curves and Surfaces", *JACM*, April 1974, 21(2), 293-310.

(8) NEWMAN, W.M. and SPROULL, R.F., *Principles of Interactive Computer Graphics.* (2nd. Ed.) McGraw-Hill, New York, 1979.

(9) GUNASEKERA, J.S., "Development of a CAD system for shaped engineering parts", *ACADS Int. Symp. on CAD/CAM*, Melbourne, Australia, Oct 1980, pp. 32-38.

Chapter 5

MODERN DIE DESIGN TECHNOLOGY

5.1 Computer Aided Engineering Approach

With the advent of computers, die design technology is currently undergoing some revolutionary changes. The traditional trial and error methods are increasingly being replaced with modern computer methods. The designer can now design and optimize a die for a given situation interactively via a computer and a graphics terminal. Computer metal flow analysis has reduced the number of iterations required to optimize the die geometry and processing parameters. Colour graphics and 3-D have enhanced the computer's ability to communicate with the designer more effectively and increase the overall productivity of the design process. Expert systems such as TRIAD have taken the guesswork out of die design and process control. Typically such systems can prompt and guide the designer to arrive at the optimum die design in a single session with the computer. The designer need not remember awkward formulae or carry out tedious calculations or make sketches of complex 3-D dies on paper. The computer provides a tremendous advantage to the designer and often prevents him making costly mistakes. The net result is shorter lead times, reduced costs and, in general, increased productivity. This chapter provides detailed descriptions of modern extrusion die design technology. Die design for other unit processes is also described briefly.

The areas covered include:- streamlined extrusion dies (the majority of this book), forging dies, plastic moulding dies and casting dies.

5.2 Design of Streamlined Extrusion Dies.

The design of streamlined dies for the extrusion of complex non-axisymmetric sections is quite complex. It is influenced by a variety of factors such as:-

*The type of extrusion process (direct, indirect or
 hydrostatic)
*extrusion temperature and pressure
*type of lubrication used (unlubricated, glass lubrication,
 grease or other compounds such as MoS_2)
*shape of product
*billet size
*press capacity and type
*extrusion ratio
*number of centres in die
*press-tool management
*die material

It is quite obvious from the foregoing that no single die
design can be used for all possible extrusion conditions.
Hence it is appropriate to support alternative die designs
depending on the given extrusion conditions. These can be
divided broadly into the following types:-

(1) Materials that are extruded in a direct process with glass
    lubrication. This group includes the extrusion of steels,
    titanium alloys and high temperature alloys.
(2) Materials not extruded in a direct process with grease or
    oil type lubricants. This group includes hard aluminium
    alloys.
(3) Materials that can be more economically extruded through
    shear-faced dies without lubrication. Soft aluminium
    alloys would fall into this category. One of the major
    problems in this area is the proper design of die land to
    give uniform flow of metal through the die and avoid
    defects due to bending and twisting of the product.
(4) Materials extruded by hydrostatic extrusion.
(5) Shapes too complex to be extruded by a streamlined die.
    This group may include aluminium alloys that are usually
    extruded into complex shapes through bridge or porthole
    dies.

5.3 Lubricated Extrusion of Aluminium Alloys

As stated earlier, the standard practice for the hot
extrusion of aluminium alloys has long been to use shear-faced
dies without lubrication. With this technique, the metal flows
by internal shear and not by sliding along the die surface. A
stationary or slow moving metal cap (known as the dead metal

zone) is formed near the flat faced die which acts like a hypothetical shaped die. The deforming metal and the dead metal zone are separated by a thin zone of intense shear as shown in Fig. 5.1.

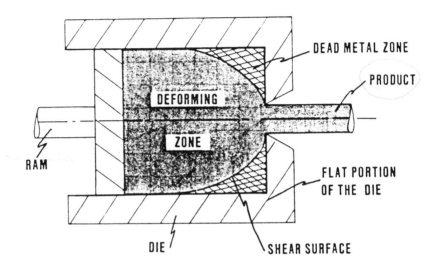

Fig. 5.1 Shear die

Thus, the resulting extrusion has a high-quality finish that requires no major surface conditioning. However, this type of extrusion operation has the following disadvantages:-

(1) Due to nonuniform metal flow, the redundant work and the extrusion pressure are high.

(2) The redundant work causes heat generation which, combined with the already high temperature necessary for extrusion, can cause ruptures on the surface of the extrusion, and even local melting in the extruded material. To overcome this problem, extrusion is performed at slow speeds, which reduces the production rate.

(3) Nonuniform metal flow results in anisotropy across the section of the extruded material.

(4) Whisker-reinforced metal matrix composites cannot be extruded without damaging the whiskers.

(5) Metal matrix composites with whiskers can be extruded without much damage to the fibres - thus preserving the mechanical properties of the extruded shape.

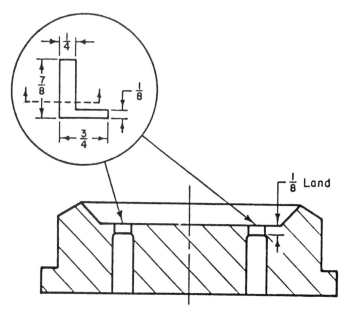

Fig. 5.2 Conical die[5]

Little work has been done concerning the lubricated
extrusion of aluminium alloys and metal matrix composites.
Nevertheless, a few articles have been published which deserve
discussion.   According to AKERET[1], by adequate lubrication
of the billet and of the container, the metal flow during
extrusion can be changed to such an extent that it would
correspond essentially to that found in cold extrusion.   The
key, of course, is proper lubrication.   Inadequate or excessive
lubrication leads to characteristic surface defects.   Tool design
and surface finish become important since these variables
influence the effectiveness of the lubricant.   Work at Battelle
(NICHOLS et al.[2]), using the conical flat die illustrated in
Fig. 5.2, has shown interesting and promising results.   Studies
conducted with 2024 alloy, a hard aluminium alloy, showed
that rounds and L-sections could be extruded at exit speeds
over 100 ft/min without surface cracking, at a billet
temperature of only 550°F.   It should be noted that these exit
speeds are approximately 5 to 10 times the exit speeds
encountered in conventional extrusion.   This study showed that
surface finish improved with increasing extrusion ratio and
with increasing extrusion speed.   For very high exit speeds,
over 200 ft/min, the surface of the extruded product showed
scoring.   It was felt that better lubrication could improve this

condition.   In general, however, the quality of the extruded rods and L-sections was comparable to that of conventionally extruded material.

Lubricated extrusion of aluminium alloys has been investigated by Russian workers KORNILOV *et al.*[3] who reported work on the experimental extrusion of fan blades from aluminium with different lubricants.   They concluded that chamfered billets, with either an aqueous suspension of MoS_2, or Cu plating (20 μm) in $CuSO_4$ and MoS_2, gave good results.

IVONOV *et al.*[4] also used the lubricated-extrusion process to extrude 0.12-inch wall tubing in a 480 ton vertical press. Tubes having 29 mm O.D. × 23 mm I.D. were successfully extruded using moderate amounts of lubrication, through a conical die with 60° included angle and a floating mandrel. Temperatures of 460° to 480° F were used and extrusion rates of 18 to 25 m/min (60 to 80 ft/min) were obtained.

NAGPAL and ALTAN[5], of Battelle's Columbus Labs., conducted the first systematic investigation into the analysis and CAD/CAM of streamlined dies.   Some of the contents reported in this monograph have been included directly from their studies.

SCHEY *et al.*[6,7] conducted lubricated extrusion of commercially pure aluminium with the aim of simulating the hydrodynamic (thick film) lubrication behaviour in extruding high-strength materials. The lubricant used in these model tests was abietic acid; only round sections were extruded with an extrusion ratio of 5:1.   Conical dies with included angles of 60°, 90°, 120° and 180° were used.   Experimental variables included extrusion temperatures, by which lubricant viscosity was controlled, extrusion speed, and a variety of secondary geometrical die variables.   The results showed that reduced extrusion pressure and excellent surface finish can be achieved by obtaining an optimum lubricant film through suitable selection of the experimental variables.

Lubricated extrusion of hard aluminium alloys by the hydrostatic extrusion process has been investigated by HORNMARK *et al.*[8].   They claimed that cold lubricated extrusion of high-strength alloys at exit speeds over 5 m/sec (about 100 times the exit speeds with conventional extrusion) is possible.   For the hard 7075 aluminium alloy, an extrusion ratio of 100:1 and surface finish and tolerances comparable to those found in cold drawing were obtained.

An interesting study of the adiabatic extrusion of hard aluminium alloys has been conducted by AKERET[9].   The important feature of this study is the suggested die profiles for lubricated extrusion of a bar with two ribs as shown in Fig. 5.3. Until now, no comparative studies have been published on the relative merits of these different designs, including their influence on extrusion pressure, uniformity of lubrication, and surface finish.

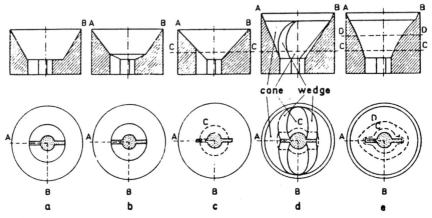

(a) Conical Flat   (b) Double Conical   (c) Conical Shape   (d) Cone and Wedge   (e) Streamlined

Fig. 5.3. Possible die designs for lubricated extrusion of a bar with two ribs[5]

GUNASEKERA et al.[10] conducted an in-depth analysis of the extrusion process for a metal-matrix composite, with SiC whiskers using streamlined and other shaped dies. These researchers developed a new technique for streamlined die design of non re-entry structural parts and also developed new techniques for the computer-aided manufacture of the dies. GEGEL et al.[11] carried out finite element analysis of the metal flow through different die geometries in order to understand the correlation of metal flow with other processing parameters such as strain, strain rate, temperature and hydrostatic stress. This work is fully described in the following chapter.

It is quite evident from the present state-of-the-art survey that lubricated extrusion of aluminium alloys is possible and has a definite potential, especially when applied to the extrusion of hard aluminum alloys and metal matrix composites. Speeds used in extrusion of soft alloys are quite high and the extrusion pressure, being relatively low, is not a limiting factor in the process design. These observations, coupled with the fact that flat-faced dies are more economical to manufacture than streamlined dies seems to suggest that lubricated extrusion of soft aluminium alloys may not be economically feasible.

However, in the extrusion of hard alloys, and metal matrix composites with fibre reinforcement, much can be gained through lubricated extrusion with streamlined dies. High extrusion speeds could be' obtained because of smaller temperature increases due to friction and redundant work. Also, lower capacity presses could be used since the required specific extrusion pressures would be less in lubricated extrusion through streamlined dies than in nonlubricated extrusion through flat-faced dies. However, the most significant benefit of the use of streamlined dies for lubricated extrusion would be in the area of P/M metal matrix composites with or without fibre reinforcement. Here, dies designed for specific purposes could be used to enhance mechanical properties of the extrudate to obtain a better surface finish, reduce defects and most importantly, impart homogeneous properties and microstructure to the product through uniform deformation.

5.4 Lubricated Extrusion of Steel and Titanium Alloys

Lubricated extrusion of titanium alloys, alloy steels, stainless steels and tool steels is, in principle, similar to the extrusion of aluminium alloys. However, in practice the steels and titanium alloys generate other problems due to higher deformation and die wear. Lubrication is commonly effected by the use of a variety of graphite and glass-based lubricants.

Commercial grease mixtures containing solid-film lubricants, such as graphite, often provide little or no thermal protection to the die; therefore, die wear in the conventional extrusion of steel and titanium alloys is very significant and results in high costs. Studies at TRW (HAVERSTRAW[12]) have demonstrated that a mixture of magnesium metaborate and graphite in water shows considerable promise as an extrusion lubricant at temperatures as high as 3500°F. Surface finishes were good in both instances[12].

5.5 The Séjournet Process

In the Séjournet process, the heated billet is commonly rolled over a bed of ground glass, or it is sprinkled with glass powder which supplies a layer of low-melting glass to the billet surface (SEJOURNET[13], HAFFNER and SEJOURNET[14] and HAVERSTRAW[12]).   Prior to insertion of the billet into the hot extrusion container, a suitable die glass lubricating system is positioned immediately ahead of the die.   This may consist of a compacted glass pad, glass wool, or both.   The prelubricated billet is quickly inserted into the container followed by appropriate followers or a dummy block, and the extrusion cycle is started, as seen in Fig. 5.4 (BYRER[15]).

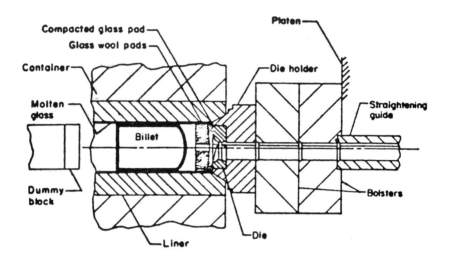

Fig. 5.4 Hot extrusion set-up using glass lubrication
(after BYRER[15])

The unique features of glass as a lubricant are its ability to soften selectively during contact with the hot billet and, at the same time, to insulate the hot-billet material from the tooling, which is usually maintained at a temperature considerably lower than that of the billet.   In extruding titanium and steel, the billet temperature is usually between 1800°F and 2300°F whereas the maximum temperature which tooling can withstand is from 900°F to 1000°F.   Thus, the only way to obtain compatibility between the very hot billet and considerably cooler tooling is to use appropriate lubricants, insulative die coating and ceramic die inserts, and to design dies to minimize tool wear.   To date, only glass lubricant has worked successfully on a production basis in extruding long lengths.

5.6 Extrusion Speed

The actual ram speed attainable during extrusion varies with alloy composition, extrusion temperature, and extrusion ratio, but is usually in the range of 200 to 300 in/min. High extrusion speeds are preferred whether grease or glass is used as the lubricant. As grease lubricants offer little protection from the high extrusion temperatures, the hot billet should be in contact with the die for as short a time as possible. With glass acting as an insulator between billet and tools, this problem is somewhat reduced. However, the basic principle of glass lubrication, i.e., glass in a state of incipient fusion flowing continuously from a reservoir, requires high extrusion speeds. With low speeds the glass reservoir may be depleted before completion of the extrusion stroke, since the melting rate of the glass is a function of time.

5.7 Die Design

Two basic types of metal flow occur during the extrusion of titanium and steel with lubrication:

(1)   Parallel metal flow in which the surface skin of the billet becomes the surface skin of the extrusion.
(2)   Shear metal flow in which the surface skin of the billet penetrates into the mass of the billet and creates a stagnant zone of metal at the die shoulder which is retained in the container as discard. Shear flow is undesirable because it prevents effective lubrication of the die and can cause interior laminations and surface defects in the extruded product.

In extrusion with grease lubricants, the common practice is to use modified flat-faced dies having a small angle and a radiused die entry. In the glass-extrusion process, the die must be designed not only to produce parallel metal flow, but also to provide a reservoir of glass on the die face. The general design employed by companies licensed for the process is a flat-faced design with a radiused entry into the die opening. During extrusion, the combination of the glass pad on the die and uniform metal flow produces a nearly conical metal flow towards the die opening.

In a study conducted by the Republic Aviation Corporation, (CHRISTIANA[16]) extrusion trials were performed on titanium alloys C-135 AMo and MS 821 to extrude L-shapes, i.e. angles.   Both glass lubricants and grease with graphite lubricants were investigated.   Glass lubrication resulted in better surface finish and die life.   The major problem with grease and graphite was maintaining sufficient lubrication over the full length of the extrusion.   A multi-hole, flat die with 20° inlet angle, seen in Fig. 5.5, produced good results.

In the same study, extrusion trials were conducted at U.S. Steel to extrude small U-shaped channels from titanium alloys.

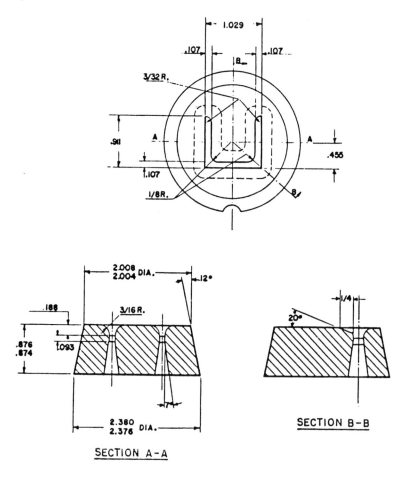

Fig. 5.5 Flat-faced die used for extruding titanium alloys
Ti-155A and C-135 AMo[5]

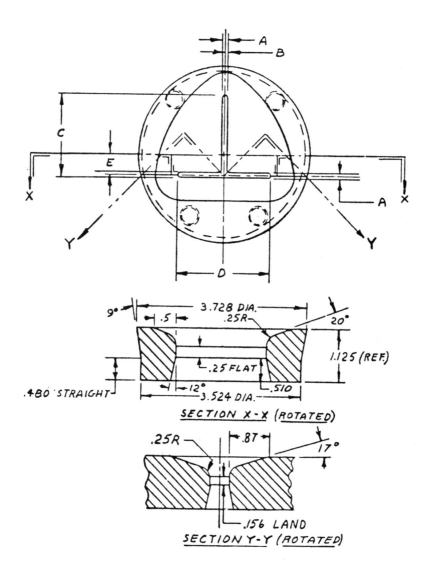

SHAPE*	A	B	C	D	E
676	.063	.0315	1.685	1.840	.410
676A	.072	.036	1.685	1.840	.410
677	.098	.049	1.050	1.840	.175

Fig. 5.6 Modified flat-faced die design used for extruding
titanium alloys with glass lubricant[5]

The conclusion of this study was that conical dies had no noticeable advantage over flat-faced dies when glass lubrication was used during the extrusion. Laminar flow was obtained with both die types. A disadvantage of conical dies with glass lubrication was the loss of much of the glass pad with the first foot of extrusion. When grease-based lubrication was used, shear-type flow occurred with both conical and flat-faced die types, but the shear cone formed was somewhat less pronounced with a conical die contour. The flat-faced die used in this study is shown in Fig. 5.5. Similar conclusions were made based on extrusion trials at H.M. Harper Company. Conical dies enhanced the metal flow, but did not retain the glass for proper lubrication. In final trials at Babcock and Wilcox Corporation, a modified flat-faced die was successfully employed for T-shape extrusion. The die used is shown in Fig. 5.6.

Similar die designs were used for extruding T-shapes of Beta III and other titanium alloys with glass lubrication. In the Séjournet process, it is usually assumed that the primary function of the die-glass pad is to lubricate the die. In a study conducted by Northrop and Harper (see SCOW and DEMPSEY[17]) on extruding "T" sections of steel, it was determined that the glass pad placed in front of the die does not lubricate the surface of the extrusion and is not necessary to produce an acceptable surface finish. The function of the die-glass pad is to provide a smooth flow pattern for the billet material. If that is the case, then better extrusions may be obtained by streamlined dies, even without a glass pad. The die used in Harper's study was quite similar to that shown in Fig. 5.6. It is interesting to note that in the optimized die-glass pad design, the amount of glass used is very much reduced and the design of the shape of the glass pad is primarily for providing streamlined flow. In another study of the extrusion of steel, a die design similar to that shown in Fig. 5.6, was used (CHRISTENSEN[18]).

An interesting conclusion was made in a study on the extrusion of Beryllium (CHRISTENSEN and WELLS[18]). In that study, it was determined that flat-faced dies are best for the glass lubricant approach, i.e. the Séjournet process, but dies with conical entry are best suited for using composite lubricants having metallic and non-glass liquid components. Based on several extrusion trials, a conical entry die was selected to encourage smooth metal flow. The dies were cast by the Shaw process by the "Duplicast Die Company of Detroit" and were finished at the "Moczik Tool and Die

Company, Detroit".

Of special importance is their conclusion quoted here. "It was apparent from past experience that the die design would have to be altered radically because of the complete change in type and method of application of lubricants. Under the Séjournet system of glass lubrication, flat-faced design was a necessity to provide the reservoir of semi-molten glass which was gradually drawn off as the billet passed the so-called 'dead zone'. With the composite lubricant technique in which the beryllium never touches the die, the metallic and liquid lubricants are applied over the entire billet surface prior to insertion into the container. This obviates the need for the reservoir provided by flat-faced dies and, in fact, dictates the need for smoother, more streamlined flow." This was accomplished best by using a conical die approach. In the study with glass lubrication, conical contour dies with varying geometries were tried. With dual lubricant systems, a curved die, as shown in Fig. 5.7, was used.

The above conclusion does not seem to apply to all situations. In extruding complex thin H-sections of Tantalum alloy (KROM[19]), better and more consistent results were obtained with the conical H-dies than the modified flat dies. Conical dies have also been used in glass-lubricated extrusion of T-shapes from TZM alloy (SANTOLI[20]), as shown diagrammatically in Fig. 5.8.

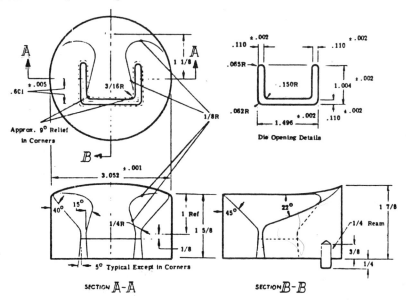

Fig. 5.7 Curved die used for extruding beryllium[5]

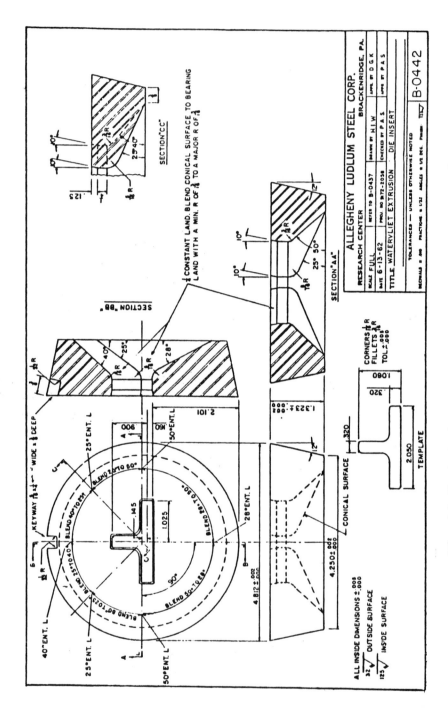

Fig. 5.8 Conical die used for extruding TZM "T" shapes[5]

The review of past studies shows that, basically, two types of dies are used for extruding steel and titanium: (a) the flat-faced die, or modified flat-faced die with radiused entry, and (b) the conical entry die. It seems that flat-faced dies, or modified flat-faced dies are used with glass lubrication with the glass pad forming the die contour at the entrance. The conical-entry die is mostly used with grease lubrication, although there is evidence, at least in extrusion of other high-strength alloys, that conical-contoured dies are also used with glass lubrication. From the review, it is obvious that in designing dies for lubricated extrusion, an important consideration, in addition to uniform flow, is the uniform distribution of lubricant on the surface of the billet.

5.8 Computer Aided Design (CAD) of Streamlined Extrusion Dies

Some of the early research work on streamlined dies was conducted by NAGPAL and ALTAN[5] at Battelle Columbus Labs. for a project conducted under the sponsorship of AMMRC and AVRADCOM. They developed computer-aided techniques for the design and manufacture of "streamlined" dies for extrusion of shapes from steels, titanium and other high temperature alloys, as illustrated in Fig. 5.9.

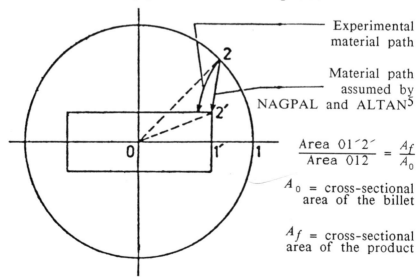

Experimental material path

Material path assumed by NAGPAL and ALTAN[5]

$$\frac{\text{Area } 01'2'}{\text{Area } 012} = \frac{A_f}{A_0}$$

A_0 = cross-sectional area of the billet

A_f = cross-sectional area of the product

Fig. 5.9 Material path along the die surface[22]

NAGPAL and ALTAN[5] performed experiments for the extrusion of non-circular sections using streamlined dies. They manufactured several streamlined dies with the aid of computer-aided techniques, assuming that the material paths along the die surface are straight.. The streamlines along the die surface in the extrusion of rectangular and "T" sections from round rods were carefully examined.

However, it was reported that, although the material path assumed is close to the actual path near the plane of symmetry, the discrepancy between the two paths becomes larger as the distance from the plane of symmetry increases, and the discrepancy also increases towards the die exit.

This discrepancy can be taken into account by the proposed die definition described below. According to Nagpal and Altan, the force of extrusion is not sensitive to higher order polynomial curves representing the die profile, so that the following third order polynomial is used in the present definition for the die profile {f(z)} to connect the points on the entry to the die with the corresponding points on the exit (see Fig. 5.10):-

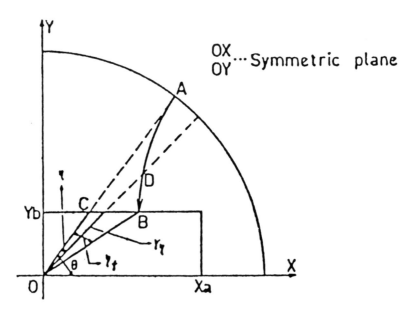

Fig. 5.10 Proposed die definition[22]

$$f(z) = a_0 + a_1 z + a_2 z^2 + a_3 z^3 \qquad (5.1)$$

where a_0', a_1', a_2 and a_3 are constants to be determined, and z is the co-ordinate along the longitudinal axis. Equation 5.1 satisfies the following boundary conditions:-

$$f(z) = R_0 \text{ at } z = 0, \; f(z) = y_n \text{ at } z = L$$

$$\frac{df(z)}{dz} = 0 \text{ at } z = 0, L \qquad (5.2)$$

where L is the die length, R_0 is the radius of the round billet and y_n is the distance from the extruding axis to the point on the perimeter of the exit shape. Substitution of the above boundary conditions in Equation 5.1 gives:-

$$f(z) = 2(R_0 - y_n)(z^3/L^3) - 3(R_0 - y_n)(z^2/L^2) + R_0 \qquad (5.3)$$

$$L \neq 0$$

Since the initial deformation of the material is very similar to that of the material in an axisymmetric extrusion, the streamline starts from the point on the periphery at entry (point A) at which it is tangential to the radius AO. Then the streamline deviates towards the final point B along the curved line AB. The deviation of the streamline can be incorporated by defining the angular change, n, as a function of z. However, at this moment, it is necessary to make an assumption for defining the form of the function n which is to be determined through optimization. Hence, n is assumed to be a function of z as follows:-

$$n = k_0 + k_1 z + k_2 z^2 \qquad (5.4)$$

where the boundary conditions are:-

$$n = 0, \; \frac{dn}{dz} = 0 \text{ at } z = 0, \; n = n_f \text{ at } z = L \qquad (5.5)$$

Substituting the boundary conditions in Equation 5.4 gives:-

$$n = n_f \frac{z^2}{L^2} \qquad (5.6)$$

where n_f is the maximum deviated angle. In the case of the extrusion of rectangular sections, y_n in Equation 5.3 is expressed as:-

$$y_n = y_b/\sin(\theta - n)$$
$$\text{or} \qquad\qquad\qquad\qquad\qquad\qquad\qquad (5.7)$$
$$y_n = x_a/\cos(\theta + n)$$

Substituting Equations 5.6 and 5.7 into Equation 5.3, the die profile function f(z) becomes:-

$$f(z) = 2\{R_0 - y_b/\sin(\theta - n_f\frac{z^2}{L^2})\}\frac{z^3}{L^3} -$$

$$3\{R_0 - y_b/\sin(\theta - n_f\frac{z^2}{L^2})\}\frac{z^2}{L^2} + R_0$$

(5.8)

or

$$f(z) = 2\{R_0 - x_a/\cos(\theta + n_f\frac{z^2}{L^2})\}\frac{z^3}{L^3} -$$

$$3\{R_0 - x_a/\cos(\theta + n_f\frac{z^2}{L^2})\}\frac{z^2}{L^2} + R_0$$

In Equation 5.8, once the angle of maximum deviation (n_f) from the angle θ on the plane of the final cross section is obtained, the die geometry can be determined numerically. This suggests that n_f might be considered as another variable in addition to the die length in the process of optimization. The die profile obtained through the proposed die definition is shown in Figs. 5.11 and 5.12.

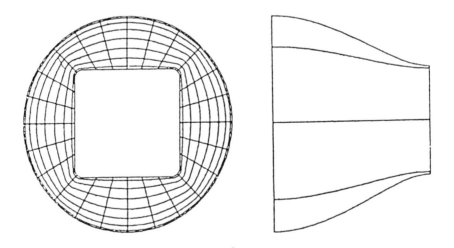

Fig. 5.11 Die profile obtained through the proposed die definition[22]

Experimental work carried out by HOSHINO[24] and finite-element simulation of the metal flow undertaken by GUNASEKERA et al.[23] have confirmed some of the above advantages of streamlined dies. Hoshino conducted a series of experiments on streamlined dies of various shapes, using lead as the model material.

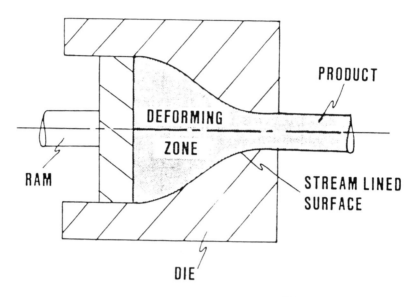

Fig. 5.12 Streamlined die[10]

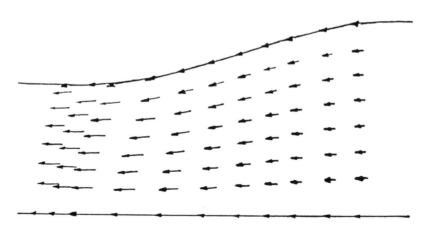

Fig. 5.13 Velocity field in streamlined extrusion
(Al 1100 at 20°C, die length = 75mm)[10]

Observations made on grid distortion and extrusion load confirm that the streamlined die with optimized geometry (die length, etc.) and proper lubrication can reduce the extrusion load and, more importantly, produce a more homogeneously deformed product.

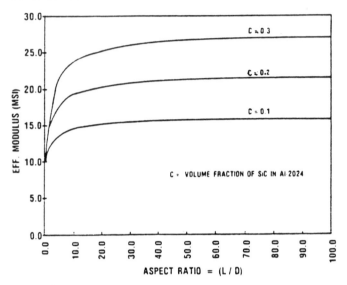

Fig. 5.14 Effective modulus as a function of aspect ratio[10]

The theoretical investigation conducted by Gunasekera *et al.*, using a rigid visco-plastic analysis of extrusion, confirmed Hoshino's experimental observations. Although this analysis was confined to the axisymmetric and plane-strain situation, the streamlined die produced more homogeneously deformed products than other dies. A typical velocity field for axisymmetric extrusion of Al 1100 at 20 °C is shown in Fig. 5.13. It can be seen that the velocity field is fairly uniform, with no abrupt velocity change within the deforming region. The main advantage of the streamlined die is that it offers smooth material flow since the surface of the die consists of smooth splines. The reduction of the extrusion force is not significant compared to the other benefits obtained when extruding metal-matrix composites with whiskers.

For the present study the material used was Al 2024 with 20 vol% SiC. This new material has a higher modulus (nearly twice that of Al 2024) when the aspect ratio of the SiC whiskers is more than 15 (see Fig. 5.14). However, the properties of the material (particularly the modulus) decrease sharply when the aspect ratio of the SiC whiskers is below 10. The use of this material can reduce the weight of a typical aircraft component by as much as 40%. The problem is, however, to extrude the complex shapes without breaking the whiskers. The conventional shear (or flat-faced) die destroys the superior mechanical properties of this material, as shown in Fig. 5.15. The streamlined die is designed in such a way that velocity changes are minimized, thus reducing the breakage of the whiskers.

5.9 Die Geometry

In non-lubricated extrusion of shapes through shear (flat-faced) dies, the deforming material shears internally during the initial stages of extrusion and forms a "dead-metal zone" on the flat face of the die. This zone acts as a streamlined die surface having a friction factor equal to one (i.e. the shear stress is equal to the shear yield stress of the material). The geometry of the dead-metal zone (a three-dimensional surface in this case) adjusts itself in such a way that the rate of energy dissipation is minimized. A similar approach was used by NAGPAL and ALTAN[5] and by GUNASEKERA and HOSHINO[21,22] concerning the geometry of complex stream-lined dies.

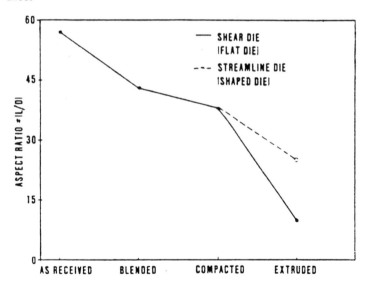

Fig. 5.15 Variation of aspect ratio during processing (Al 2024 with 20 vol% SiC whiskers)[10]

In lubricated extrusion, the die should provide a smooth transition from round billet to the final extruded shape without abrupt velocity change (or discontinuity). In addition,

the design of the die geometry should be such that the
material undergoes minimal redundant deformation and also
exits from the die without twisting or bending. This
requirement is satisfied if the material leaving the die has a
constant axial velocity profile.

The concept of die design used by these researchers is
illustrated in Fig. 5.16. Here sectors of the billet are mapped
onto corresponding sectors at the exit side, with the same
extrusion ratio being maintained. Hence:-

$$\text{Area OPQ/Area OP}'\text{Q}' = R = \text{Area OPR/Area OP}'\text{R}'$$

where R is the extrusion ratio. This criterion ensures a
uniform velocity profile at the exit of the die. Thereafter,
splines of any order are used to fit the entry and exit
sections. The method fails, however, for sections which are
re-entrant, as shown in Figs. 5.16 and 5.17. The reason for
this failure is that some radial lines passing through the axis
of extrusion (such as OP) cut the perimeter of the product at
more than one point (e.g. P', P'', and P''').

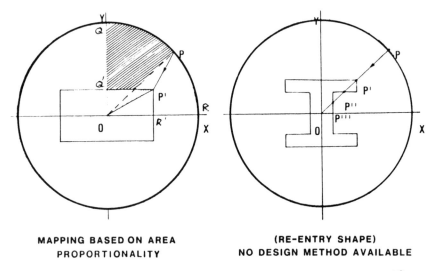

MAPPING BASED ON AREA   (RE-ENTRY SHAPE)
PROPORTIONALITY   NO DESIGN METHOD AVAILABLE

Fig. 5.16 Limitations of previous methods of die design[10]

A new technique has been developed to overcome this
problem. Essentially, the method consists of transforming the
area-mapping technique to a perimeter- (line-) mapping technique by use of Stokes' theorem. The method is illustrated in
Fig. 5.17. For re-entry sections the local line integral may

become negative but can be re-distributed to neighbouring areas with little difficulty. For product sections having one perimeter, the method applies even if the section has re-entrants.

Referring to Fig. 5.16, a sector in the billet such as OPQ can be mapped onto a section OP´Q´ in the entry section such that:-

$$\text{Area OPQ/Area OP´Q´} = R$$

Stokes' theorem can be used to convert this area-mapping technique to a line-integral technique, as follows:-

$$\int\int_S (\nabla \times A)\,\mathrm{d}s = \int_l A\,\mathrm{d}l$$

where $\underline{A}$ is a vector function, i.e.:-

$$\underline{A} = \underline{A_1}i + \underline{A_2}j + \underline{A_3}k,$$

and:-

$$\nabla = i\frac{\partial}{\partial x} + j\frac{\partial}{\partial y} + k\frac{\partial}{\partial z}$$

in general.

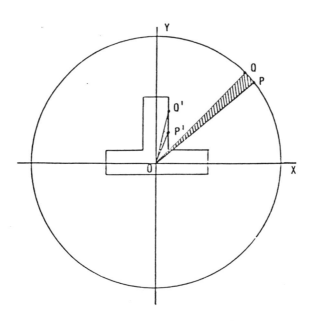

Fig. 5.17 New concept of die design for extrusion[10]

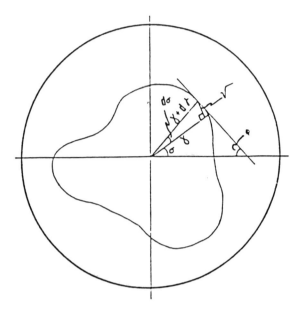

Fig. 5.18 Stokes' Theorem applied to die design[10]

Referring to Fig. 5.18, the line integral for this particular case reduces to:-

$$\frac{1}{2} \int \gamma \, \sin \, \nu \, \, ds$$

Thus,

Area OPQ → Area OP´Q´

becomes   Line PQ → Line P´Q´

The above analysis was used by GUNASEKERA[22] to develop a CAD/CAM package for die design known as STREAM.   STREAM is capable of generating straight (conical), convex, concave, and parabolic die shapes, in addition to streamlined die shapes.   With advancements in the extrusion industry there is a need to design complex dies from arbitrary shaped or preformed billets to complex products. The program STREAM was modified by MEHTA[25,26] for this application.   The package was further modified by GUNASEKERA, MEHTA, and WALTERS[27] to design part-conical, part-streamlined dies.   Several dies have been designed and manufactured using this package.   One die geometry starts from a rectangular billet and ends in a complex shape as shown in Fig. 5.19. This die was designed

for General Electric Co, USA, and manufactured and used by
Ontario Forge, USA.   A second die (Fig. 5.20) was designed
at Ohio University using this package on the Intergraph CAD
system and manufactured by Cameron Forge Co., Texas, USA.

Fig. 5.19 Electrode for a streamlined die (Rectangular billet
to complex product)[26]

Fig. 5.20 Part-conical, part-streamlined die (inside view)[27]

REFERENCES

(1) AKERET, R., "Research in the Nonferrous Metal Product Industry, Part XX, Effects of Lubricating the Container on the Extrusion of Aluminium and Aluminium Alloys", (in German), *Z. Metallkunde* 1964, **55(10)**, 570–573.

(2) NICHOLS, D.E., BYRER, T.G. and SABROFF, A.M., "Lubricated Extrusion of 2024 Aluminium Alloy Using Conical and Conical–Flat Dies", *Summary Report to Battelle Development Corp.*, Columbus, Ohio, 1970.

(3) KORNILOV, V.V., NEDOUROV, Y.S., ANTONOV, E.A., ABROSIMOV, A.I. and SMIRNOV, G.A., "Experimental Extrusion of Aluminium–Alloy Fan Blades", (in Russian), *Kuznechno–Shtampovochnoye Proizvodstvo* 1970, **10**, 15.

(4) IVONOV, I.I., RAKHMANOV, N.S., MOLODCHININ, E.V., MOLODCHININA, A.I., and MEDVEDEVA, R.D., "Extrusion of Thin–Walled D 16 Alloy Tubes on a Vertical Press", *The Soviet Journal of Nonferrous Metals* 1968, **9(7)**, 100.

(5) NAGPAL, V., and ALTAN, T., "Computer–Aided Design and Manufacturing for Extrusion of Aluminium, Titanium and Steel Structural Parts (Phase 1)", *AVSCOM Report No. 76–12*, Battelle Columbus Labs., 1976.

(6) SCHEY, J.A., WALLACE, P.W., and KULKARNI, K.M., "Thick–Film Lubrication in Hot Extrusion", U.S. Air Force Materials Laboratory, May, 1968, *Technical Report AFML–TR–68–141.*

(7) WALLACE, P.W., KULKARNI, K.M., and SCHEY, J.A., "Thick–Film Lubrication in Model Extrusions with Low Extrusion Ratios", *Journal of the Institute of Metals*, 1972, **(100)**, 78.

(8) HORNMARK, N., NILSSON, J.O.H. and MILLS, C.P., "Quintus Hydrostatic Extrusion", *Metal Forming* 1970, **(37)**, 227.

(9) AKERET, R. and STRATMAN, P.M., "Unconventional Extrusion Processes for the Harder Aluminium Alloys Part I and II", *Light Metal Age* 1973, April, 6–10, June, 15–18.

(10) GEGEL, H.L., MALAS, J.C., GUNASEKERA, J.S., and DORAIVELU, S.M., "CAD/CAM of Extrusion Dies for Extrusion of P/M Materials", *Proc. of the American Soceity of Metals Congress*, 1982, pp. 1-9

(11) GEGEL, H.L. and GUNASEKERA, J.S., "Computer-Aided Design of Dies by Metal-Flow Simulations", AGARD, NATO, Paper No. 137, France 1984, pp. 8-1 - 8-8.

(12) HAVERSTRAW, R.C., "High Temperature Extrusion Lubricants", TRW Electro–Mechanical Division of TRW, Inc., Cleveland, Ohio, 1964, *Report ML–TDR–64–256*.

(13) SÉJOURNET, J. and DELCROIX, J., "Glass Lubricant in the Extrusion of Steel", *Lubrication Engineering*, 1955, (11), 389.

(14) HAFFNER,E.K.L. and SÉJOURNET,J., "The Extrusion of Steel", *Journal of the Iron and Steel Institute*, June, 1960, 145.

(15) BYRER, T.G., *et al.*, "Design Guide for Use of Structural Shapes in Aircraft Applications", Battelle Labs., Columbus, Ohio, September, 1973, *Technical Report AFML–TR–73–211*.

(16) CHRISTIANA, J.J., "Improved Methods for the Production of Titanium Alloy Extrusions", Republic Aviation Corp., *Final Technical Engineering Report* 1963, *ASD Project: 7–556*.

(17) SCOW, A.L. and DEMPSEY, P.E., "Production Processes for Extruding, Drawing and Heat Treating Thin Steel Tee Sections", October, 1968, *Technical Report AFML–TR–68–293*.

(18) CHRISTENSEN, L.M. and WELLS, R.R., "Program for the Development of Extruded Beryllium Shapes", Northrop Corp., June 1962, *ASD Technical Report 62-7-644*.

(19) KROM, R.R., "Extruding and Drawing Tantalum Alloys to Complex Thin H–Sections", Nuclear Metals, Division of Textron, Inc., *Technical Report AFML–TR–66–119*.

(20) SANTOLI, P.A., "Molybdenum Alloy Extrusion Development Program", Allegheny Ludlum Steel Corp. May 1963, *Tech. Doc. Rep. ASD–TDR–63–593*.

(21) HOSHINO, S. and GUNASEKERA, J.S., "An Upper–Bound Solution for the Extrusion of Square Section from Round Bar through Converging Dies", *Proc. 21st Int. Machine Tool Design and Research Conf.*, Swansea, England, 1980, 97–105.

(22) GUNASEKERA, J.S. and HOSHINO, S., "Extrusion of Noncircular Sections through Shaped Dies", *Annals Int. Inst. Prod. Eng. Res. (CIRP)* 1980, 29, 141.

(23) GUNASEKERA, J.S., GEGEL, H.L., MALAS, J.C., and DORAIVELU, S.M., "Computer Aided Process Modeling of Hot Forging and Extrusion of Aluminum Alloys", Annals of CIRP, Vol. 31, No. 1, 1982, pp. 131-136.

(24) HOSHINO, S., "Extrusion of Non–Axisymmetric Sections through Converging Dies", *Ph.D. Thesis*, 1981, Monash Univ. Australia.

(25) MEHTA, B.V., "Computer Aided Design of Streamlined Dies", *Masters' Thesis*, Ohio University, Athens, Ohio, March 1988.

(26) MEHTA, B.V. and GUNASEKERA, J.S., "Integration of Design and Manufacturing", IGUG, Las Vegas, Nevada, Oct 11-14, 1988.

(27) GUNASEKERA, J.S., MEHTA, B.V., and WALTERS, J., "Computer Aided Design of Part Conical-Part Streamlined Die", *ASM International*, Columbus, Ohio, Nov 1-4, 1988.

Chapter 6

ANALYTICAL MODELLING

6.1 Introduction

This chapter is confined to the analytical modelling of metal forming processes since that topic plays a very important role in the areas of die design and metal forming equipment. It is important to understand that the determination of forming (or processing) variables, such as forming forces, power, stresses and extent of deformation is one of the key initial steps in the design of forming dies. Modelling techniques for extrusion die design and present-day applications for analysis of complex extrusion processes will be largely discussed in this chapter.

Extensive theoretical and experimental work in the area of metal plastic deformation have resulted in a number of useful models:-

1. Slab method
2. Upper bound method
3. Uniform plastic deformation energy method
4. Slip-line field solutions
5. Finite element method
6. Viscoplasticity method of solution
7. Experimental solutions

Two powerful and widely used methods, slab and upper bound methods, will be discussed in this section, as applied to extrusion dies. However, it should be noted that the slab method and upper bound method can be applied equally well to other metal forming processes such as forging, rolling, coining, upset welding etc.

6.2 History of Development – Principal Contributors

Many of the major contributions to the development of analytical models for metal-forming processes came in the second half of the twentieth century. SIEBEL and FANGMEIER[1] apparently first presented an analytical method for calculating the extrusion energy. SIEBEL[2] extended the energy (or work-of-deformation) method of analysis to processes other than extruding. This method is still widely used for solving general plastic-flow problems.

More rigorous mathematical treatments for the case of extruding in plane strain were developed by HILL[3]. These were based on Hencky slip-line field solutions and have been applied extensively by PRAGER and HODGE[4], GREEN[5] and BISHOP[6]. Later JOHNSON[7] and KUDO[8] applied upper bound methods to various extrusion problems and have published a variety of solutions of different conditions of extruding. HOFFMAN and SACHS[9] drew attention to the fact that the extrusion problem can be solved by the slab method of analysis.

GUNASEKERA and HOSHINO[10] developed analytical methods for extrusion based on streamlined dies, extrusion of polygonal sections, non-circular sections and various other complex geometrical sections and die surfaces. Also, Gunasekera implemented slab method models in CAD/CAM packages for extrusion die design and analysis.

In the case of forging, Prandtl analyzed the compression of an ideal perfectly-plastic solid in plane strain between rough dies and obtained rigorous solutions for the stress distribution and average forging pressure. His solutions were later carefully reconsidered by HILL[11], GREEN[12], ALEXANDER[13] and BISHOP[14]. Some more approximate solutions were also later proposed by SIEBEL[15], NADAI[16], SCHROEDER and WEBSTER[17] and others. However, perhaps the most notable contribution came from KOBAYASHI et al.[18] who proposed the slab method of solution for complex forging processes. Many other important contributions came from Johnson and Kudo who applied the upper bound approach to forging processes. Another major breakthrough came from Battelle Labs, Columbus, where an interactive CAD package called DIEFORG was developed for the design and manufacture of forging dies.

6.3 Slab Method for Extrusion of Rods[19]

The slab method is becoming increasingly popular for analyzing extrusion problems.

Let D_b = Dia. of billet being extruded
     D_a = Dia. of extruded workpiece

Consider the extrusion of a cylindrical billet through a conical section as shown in Fig. 6.1. The state of stress in the slab is given in Fig. 6.2 and the Mohr's circle in Fig. 6.3. The analysis can be applied to three distinct cases:

(1)   the coefficient of friction $\mu = 0$ and $\alpha \to 0$
(2)   the coefficient of friction $\mu \neq 0$ and $\alpha \neq 0$, but sticking does not occur
(3)   the frictional drag stress along the conical surface is equal to the yield shear resistance of the billet material.

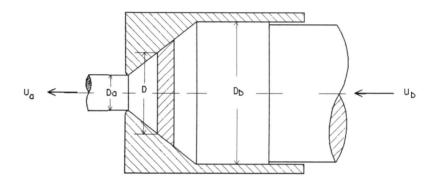

Fig. 6.1 Diagrammatic sketch of tapered-die extrusion process

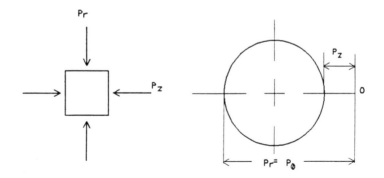

Fig. 6.2 State of stress   Fig. 6.3 Mohr's circle

For condition (1) the conical section may be considered real or imaginary. For condition (2) the conical section may be real and in (3) it is approaching a primary operation at increased temperatures, in which the conical surface may be that between the billet metal and that of the locked-in metal at the die corner.

The analysis of an extrusion problem by the slab method is quite simple when plane-strain conditions are assumed. Extrusion problems of sheet or strip can readily be handled in this manner. Unfortunately, these examples are not representative of the majority of real industrial extrusion problems, for the billet or slug normally has a cylindrical shape. This at once poses problems since, in addition to the unknown stress components σ_1 and σ_2, the unknown hoop stress σ_θ must be added.

HAAR and VON KARMAN[20] have tried to avoid this impasse for axisymmetrical problems, but it has been possible to formulate a more exact relationship among the stresses. It is assumed that in all forming problems handled by the slab method, which involve flow through conical dies, the state of stress is spherical. Hence the hoop stress and the radial stress are assumed to be equal to each other. This assumption will obviously introduce errors of unknown magnitude and the accuracy of the solutions will improve only when the cone angle is small and the coefficient of friction is small.

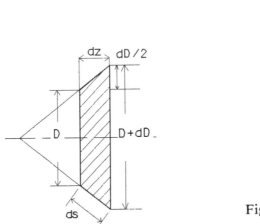

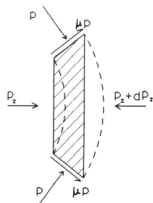

Fig. 6.4 Free-body diagram

Fig. 6.5 Geometrical relationship between dz, ds and dD

Consider the static equilibrium of the forces acting on the shaded element of Fig. 6.1 as shown in the free-body diagram of Fig. 6.4. The equation expressing static equilibrium in the z-direction is given by:-

$$\sum F_z = -(p_z+dp_z)(D+dD)^2(\pi/4) + p_z\pi D^2/4 + p_\alpha\pi Dds \sin \alpha +$$

$$\mu p_\alpha\pi Dds \cos \alpha = (6.1)$$

Equation 6.1 can be simplified by recognizing the geometrical condition along the die surface shown in Fig. 6.5 which is given by:-

$$ds \sin \alpha = dz \tan \alpha = d(D/2),$$
$$ds \cos \alpha = dz = d(D/2)/\tan \alpha \qquad (6.2)$$

In order to express Equation 6.1 in integral form, however, the instantaneous yield condition must be examined. The effective stress for the present case in which $\sigma_\theta = \sigma_r$ reduces to:-

$$\bar{\sigma} = \pm(\sigma_r - \sigma_z) = \pm(p_z - p_r) \qquad (6.3)$$

and the plasticity equation for the r-direction demands that:-

$$\frac{dr}{r} = \frac{d\bar{\epsilon}}{\bar{\sigma}}\left[\sigma_r - \frac{1}{2}(\sigma_z + \sigma_\theta)\right] = \frac{d\bar{\epsilon}}{\bar{\sigma}}\frac{(\sigma_r - \sigma_z)}{2} \qquad (6.4)$$

Furthermore, since dr/r is negative in the positive flow direction and $d\bar{\sigma}/\bar{\sigma}$ is always a positive number, it is necessary also that $(\sigma_z - \sigma_r)$ be negative.

It follows, therefore, that:-

$$\sigma_z - \sigma_r = p_r - p_z = \bar{\sigma} \qquad (6.5)$$

With reference to Mohr's circle:-

$$p_\alpha = p_r = p_\theta \qquad (6.6)$$

and substitution of the yield condition $\bar{\sigma}$ given by Equation 6.3 results in:-

$$p_\alpha = p_z + \bar{\sigma} \qquad (6.7)$$

Substituting into Equation 6.4 in terms of differentials, we obtain:-

$$\frac{dp_z}{\mu p_z \cot \alpha + (1 + \mu \cot \alpha)\bar{\sigma}} = 2\frac{dD}{D} \qquad (6.8)$$

which can be re-written as:-

$$\frac{dp_z}{B p_z + (1 + B)\bar{\sigma}} = 2\frac{dD}{D} \qquad (6.9)$$

where $B = \mu \cot \alpha$.

Case 1.

For the extrusion condition in which $\mu = 0$, $B = 0$ and in which $\alpha \to 0$, Equation 6.9 reduces to:-

$$dp_z = 2\bar{\sigma} \frac{dD}{D} \qquad (6.10)$$

which can be integrated to give:-

$$p_z = \int_{D_a}^{D_b} 2\bar{\sigma} \frac{dD}{D} = \int_{\bar{\epsilon}_b}^{\bar{\epsilon}_a} \bar{\sigma} d\bar{\epsilon} \qquad (6.11)$$

Case 2.

For the more general case of $\mu \neq 0$ and $\alpha \neq 0$ Equation 6.9 can be integrated at constant $\bar{\sigma}$ to give:-

$$\frac{1}{B} \ln[Bp_z + (1 + B)\bar{\sigma}] = 2 \ln D + \ln C \qquad (6.12a)$$

or:-

$$[Bp_z + (1 + B)\bar{\sigma}]^{1/B} = D^2 C \qquad (6.12b)$$

Evaluating the boundary condition at section (a) of Fig. 6.1 we see that $p_z = p_{za} = 0$ when $D = D_a$, which results in:-

$$C = \frac{[(1 + B)\bar{\sigma}]^{1/B}}{D_a^2} \qquad (6.13)$$

Substitution of C of Equations 9 and 8 and simplifying gives the axial pressure:-

$$p_z = \bar{\sigma} \left[\frac{1 + B}{B}\right] \left[\left[\frac{D}{D_a}\right]^{2B} - 1\right] \qquad (6.14)$$

Case 3.

Substitution of $\mu = 1/\sqrt{3}$ and $\alpha = 45°$ into B gives:-

$$B = \mu \cot \alpha = 1/\sqrt{3} \qquad (6.15)$$

B can be substituted into Equation 6.13 to get the C value in this case.

In the case of the slab method for determining extrusion pressure, the average pressure p_{ave} can be obtained by assuming an average $\bar{\sigma}$ value.

6.4 Upper Bound Solution for Extrusion of Rods

Fig. 6.6 depicts the analysis of a plane strain extrusion problem, which uses one of Johnson's upper bounds. Fig. 6.6(a) describes an assumed plastic region given by the triangle ACB, and the velocity discontinuities on line BC and line CA are indicated by the streamline. The corresponding hodograph appears in Fig. 6.6(b). The equation for the average extrusion pressure, following Johnson, is given by:-

$$\frac{p_{ave}}{\sigma} = \frac{2}{\sqrt{3}} \left[\frac{BC}{D} \overline{bc} + \frac{CA}{D} \overline{ca} + \frac{AB}{D} \overline{ab} \right]$$ (6.16)

where BC and CA are the lengths of lines in Fig. 6(a) and bc and ca are lengths of lines in the hodograph of Fig. 6(b). The so-called best solution, based on minimum energy, is obtained by varying angle α, keeping θ constant, which shifts the point B to B´, to B´´, etc., until the minimum of p_{ave} is obtained.   Conversely, angle θ may also be varied until p_{ave} becomes a minimum.   This condition is shown in Fig. 6.6(c) with θ at about 30° at which $p_{ave}/\overline{\sigma} = 2.95$, its minimum value.

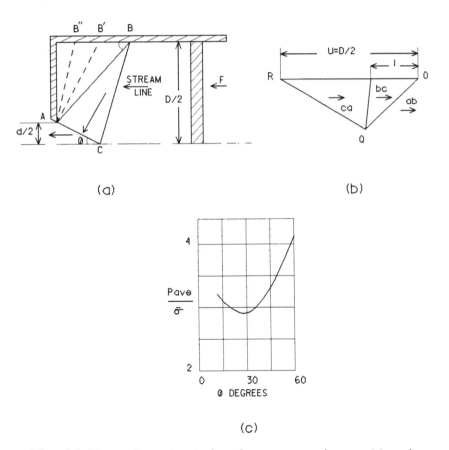

(a)   (b)

(c)

Fig. 6.6 Upper-bound solution for an extrusion problem in plane strain. (a) Simplified slip-line field, (b) Hodograph. (c) Plot to determine best solution

6.5 Advanced Analytical Techniques for Complex Extrusion Problems

Slab and upper bound methods for 2-D extrusion have been discussed in the previous sections. Most of these extrusion processes are carried out using flat-faced dies or so-called square dies under hot conditions with or without lubricants. But, for certain important applications it may not be possible to use flat-faced dies. The only solution is to resort to converging dies, with streamlined surfaces, because of their inherent advantages.

In the case of extrusion or drawing where the exit cross-section is different in shape from that at entry, the material flow does not remain on the same radial plane which contains the longitudinal axis, so that a 3-D approach is necessary.

The upper bound method giving equations for the analysis of extrusion or the direct drawing of regular polygonal sections starting from a round bar stock, proposed by HOSHINO and GUNASEKERA[10], is discussed here. The major advantage of this method is that it only requires the establishment of the generic streamline of a particle in a three-dimensional coordinate system.

6.5.1 *Introduction*

Upper bound solutions for the extrusion and the drawing of regular polygonal sections from cylindrical billets through straight converging dies, where the die surface comprises straight streamlines, have been successfully demonstrated by GUNASEKERA and HOSHINO[22]. These dies would produce changes of flow-direction at inlet and outlet of the dies. These were taken into account as velocity discontinuities. However, close observation of the dead metal zone reveals that the profile of the dead metal zone is, in general, a shaped envelope which minimizes the redundant shear, as shown schematically in Fig. 6.7. This profile might be considered as the best one under the given conditions where sticking friction occurs along the interface between the workpiece and the dead metal zone. For this reason, it becomes very important to consider curved dies as against straightly converging dies for the extrusion or drawing of sections.

In this section, previous concepts are directly extended to curved dies for the extrusion of regular polygonal and rectangular sections. The emphasis here is on the analysis of "the streamlined die," though the method to be discussed is

also applicable to other curved dies such as concave and
convex shaped dies. The die surface of "the streamlined die"
is constructed by smooth curved streamlines with zero gradient
along the extruding direction at the entry and the exit of the
die.

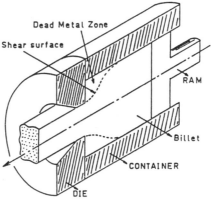

Fig. 6.7 The formation of the dead metal zone in extrusion
through a flat-faced die

6.5.2 *Streamlined Dies*

From a practical point of view, one of the major drawbacks of the use of streamlined dies for the drawing of
cylindrical bars is that the diameter of the bar has to be
controlled to a fine tolerance so as not to produce shearing of
the material at the inlet of the die. Despite this drawback,
the streamlined die, which might be considered as a derivative
of "the sigmoidal die," has such attractive features as to
reduce the reforming stress and more importantly to improve
the product quality.

RICHMOND and DEVENPECK[23] first proposed the
sigmoidal die as an ideal shape of die for the frictionless
drawing of an ideal rigid-perfectly plastic strip. Theoretically,
this die requires the minimal forming stress and produces
homogeneous deformation. It has actually been shown by
DEVENPECK and RICHMOND[24] that the sigmoidal die can
produce better mechanical properties of the product such as in
fatigue life and ductility at least under well lubricated
conditions, when compared with other straight, concave and
convex shaped dies. However, the theoretically ideal die has
a relatively large surface area, resulting in an increase of the
frictional work done. Also, HILL[25] pointed out that many
different streamlined profiles could be designed for a given
reduction of area and in consequence the die profile cannot be

uniquely determined. For these reasons RICHMOND and MORRISON[26] proposed a drawing die of minimum length, assuming again a friction-free die surface. DEVENPECK[27] has tested the efficiency of this die and concluded that a significant characteristic of die profile which minimizes structural damage and work is a zero-entrance angle. He also concluded that reducing the angle of the exit also appears desirable and thus consideration should be given to the ideal die which has zero exit angle as well as zero entry angle.

The above conclusions raised by Devenpeck have been incorporated by the present researchers in their analysis of the extrusion of non-circular sections. Other researchers such as CHEN and LING[33] and AVITZUR[36] have developed upper-bound solutions to extrusion through straight and curved dies. FRISCH and MATA-PIETRI[34] and MATA-PIETRI and FRISCH[35] performed experiments using these dies and obtained good agreement with the theoretical results. However, the analyses were limited to axisymmetric extrusions. NAGPAL and ALTAN[28] demonstrated the utility of the dual stream functions to obtain an upper bound solution for the extrusion of an elliptical cross-section from a cylindrical billet through streamlined dies. Their concept was later extended by NAGPAL[29] to the deformation problem of rectangular sections from other rectangular bars. In contrast, YANG and LEE[30] proposed the conformal mapping approach to find a kinemat-ically admissible velocity field for extrusion through concave and convex shaped dies where geometrical similarity is preserved thoughout the deformation. This method eliminated any restriction of cross-sectional shape of sections. YANG, KIM and LEE[31] also analyzed the extrusion of a helical section from cylindrical bars through straightly converging dies, and their method is in principle applicable to other curved dies.

However, these methods, discussed above, still involve limitations on the geometry of the die and it is difficult to apply their methods to the die geometries analyzed here. The explanation of the present method follows in the next section.

6.5.3 Velocity Field

The following assumptions are required to construct the kinematically admissible velocity field for the extrusion of regular polygonal sections from cylindrical billets.

1.   The material of the billet passing through sector OEG (in Fig. 6.8) at the die entry goes through triangle LFH at

the die exit, preserving the extrusion (or the drawing ratio).

2.   Stream surface OEFL consists of a number of curved streamlines which start from a point (say E') at the entry and end at a corresponding point (say F') at the exit maintaining the proportionality of the position.

The above assumptions are illustrated in Fig. 6.8.   As mentioned in the previous section, the present attempt is to produce the die configuration which requires no energy dissipation at the entry and the exit of die.   Also, it has been reported, by NAGPAL and ALTAN[28] that the extrusion force is not sensitive to higher order polynomial curves representing the die profile.   Therefore, for simplicity of the present analysis, streamlines are represented by cubic curves satisfying the smooth entry and exit of the material flow.

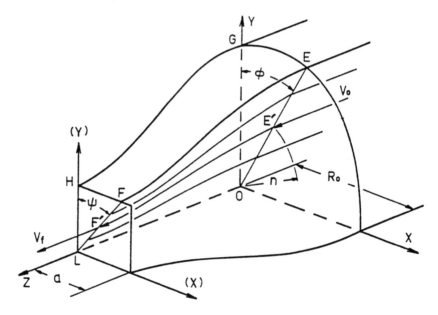

Fig. 6.8 Proposed kinematically admissible velocity field for regular polygonal sections

Any coordinate along stream-line E'F' in Fig. 6.8 is formulated in a Cartesian co-ordinate system as follows:-

$$x = f_1(z) = b_1 z^3 + b_2 z^2 + b_3 z + b_4$$

$$y = f_2(z) = c_1 z^3 + c_3 z + c_4 \qquad (6.17)$$

$$z = z$$

where b_i and c_i (i = 1,2,3 and 4) are constants determined by the boundary conditions. Consider that this streamline does not produce any abrupt change of flow direction along the extrusion axis at the entry and the exit of die, the boundary conditions are given for equation 6.17 as:-

$$
\left.
\begin{aligned}
x &= n \sin \varphi & \frac{\partial x}{\partial z} &= 0 \\
y &= n \cos \varphi & \frac{\partial y}{\partial z} &= 0
\end{aligned}
\right\} \text{at } z = 0
$$

$$
\left.
\begin{aligned}
x &= \frac{n}{R_0} a \tan \varphi & \frac{\partial x}{\partial z} &= 0 \\
y &= \frac{n}{R_0} a & \frac{\partial y}{\partial z} &= 0
\end{aligned}
\right\} \text{at } z = L
$$

(6.18)

where:-

$$
\tan \psi = \frac{N}{\pi} \tan \left[\frac{\pi}{N}\right] \cdot \varphi
$$
$$
= c\varphi
$$

R_0 is the radius of billet, a is the half side length of product cross-section, N is the number of sides in regular polygon, L is the length of die, n is the distance from the axis to an arbitrary point E' at the die entry, and φ and ψ are the angles between the plane of symmetry and the stream surface at entry and exit of the die respectively. Substitution of these boundary conditions into Equation 6.17 gives:-

$$
x = n \sin \varphi + n\left[\frac{a}{R_0}c\varphi - \sin \varphi\right]\left[3\left[\frac{z}{L}\right]^2 - 2\left[\frac{z}{L}\right]^3\right]
$$
$$
y = n \cos \varphi + n\left[\frac{a}{R_0} - \cos\varphi\right]\left[3\left[\frac{z}{L}\right]^2 - 2\left[\frac{z}{L}\right]^3\right]
$$
(6.19)

$$z = z$$

Equation 6.19 can be rewritten in the following form:-

$$
x = n \sin \varphi + n\left[\frac{a}{R_0}c\varphi - \sin \varphi\right] f(z)
$$
$$
y = n \cos \varphi + n\left[\frac{a}{R_0} - \cos\varphi\right] f(z)
$$
(6.20)

$$z = z$$

where:-
$$
\begin{aligned}
f(z) &= 0 \text{ at } z = 0 \\
f(z) &= 1 \text{ at } z = L
\end{aligned}
$$
(6.21)

In the present analysis, function f is represented by the following cubic curve:-

$$
f = f(z) = 3\left[\frac{z}{L}\right]^2 - 2\left[\frac{z}{L}\right]^3
$$
(6.22)

Equation 6.20 describes not only the co-ordinates inside the plastically deforming region but also the relationship between the Cartesian and n, φ, z coordinate systems. Although the present analysis employs the cubic curve, represented by Equation 6.22, for the description of the die profile and the assumed streamlines of particles, it should be stated that, in Equation 6.20 function f can be any general function of z provided the function satisfies the boundary conditions in Equation 6.21.

Assuming that the plastically deforming zone is bounded by shear planes at the entry and the exit of die, and utilizing the determinant of the Jacobian of Equation 6.20, the velocity components for imcompressible material are determined as:-

$$V_x = \frac{n\left[(a/R_0)c\varphi - \sin \varphi \right]}{g(\varphi,z)} \cdot V_0$$

$$V_y = \frac{n\left[(a/R_0) - \cos \varphi \right]}{g(\varphi,z)} \cdot V_0 \qquad (6.23)$$

$$V_z = \frac{1}{g(\varphi,z)} \cdot V_0$$

where:-

$$g(\varphi,z) = \begin{array}{l} \left[(1-f)^2 + c(af/R_0)^2 \right] + \\ \left[c(1-f)(af/R_0) \right]\varphi \sin \varphi + \\ \left[(1+c)(1-f)(af/R_0) \right] \cos \varphi \end{array}$$

Strain-rate components, expressed by the following tensor form, can easily be found with the aid of coordinate transformation:-

$$\dot{\varepsilon}_{ij} = \frac{1}{2} \left[\frac{\partial V_i}{\partial x_j} + \frac{\partial V_j}{\partial x_i} \right] \qquad (6.24)$$

It is apparent that the velocity field formed by Equation 6.23 satisfies the velocity boundary condition, i.e. the volume continuity of material at the inlet and outlet of the die. This velocity (or strain-rate) field has also been proved to satisfy the incompressibility condition (HOSHINO[32]). Hence the proposed velocity model fulfills the stringent requirement for the construction of a kinematically admissible condition.

6.5.4 Upper Bound Solution

Since the streamlined die produces no velocity discontinuities at the velocity boundaries, the upper limit to the total power consumption (J^*), required to deform cylindrical billets to regular polygonal sections through this die, is represented as the sum of the power consumed due to the plastic deformation (W_i) and due to the die surface friction (W_s). Considering the symmetry of the die geometry, J^* is obtained as:-

$$J^* = 2N.[W_i + W_s] \qquad (6.25)$$

where:-

$$W_i = \frac{2}{\sqrt{3}}\sigma_0 \int_V \left[\frac{1}{2}\varepsilon_{ij}\varepsilon_{ij}\right]^{\frac{1}{2}} dV$$

$$= \frac{2}{\sqrt{3}}\sigma_0 \int_0^L \int_0^{\varphi_m} \int_0^{R_0} \left[\frac{1}{2}\varepsilon_{ij}\varepsilon_{ij}\right]^{\frac{1}{2}} \left|\det J\right| \, dn d\varphi dz$$

$$W_s = m\frac{\sigma_0}{\sqrt{3}}\int_{S_3} \left|\Delta v_3\right| \, dS_3$$

$$= m\frac{\sigma_0}{\sqrt{3}}\int_0^L \int_0^{\varphi_m} [V_x^2 + V_y^2 + V_z^2]_{n=R_0}^{n=\frac{1}{2}} \cdot \frac{1}{\cos\alpha}\frac{\partial(x,z)}{\partial(n,z)} \, d\varphi \, dz$$

φ_m is the maximum angle of inclination of the die surface element with respect to the projected surface of the element on to the x-z plane. θ_m is the maximum value of the angle determined by the symmetry of the die shape, and det j is the determinant of the Jacobian of Equation 6.20. Knowing the velocity and the strain-rate components, and the co-ordinate transformation equation, the volume and surface integration are numerically carried out for given values of the yield stress of the material, θ_0 and constant frictional factor, (m) to obtain the total power consumption. The power computed can be converted to the average pressure (P_{ave}) and the relative stress (R_s), as follows:-

$$P_{ave} = \frac{J^*}{\pi R_0^2 . V_0} \qquad (6.26)$$

$$R_s = \frac{P_{ave}}{\sigma_0} \qquad (6.27)$$

The actual die length (L) is also reduced to the relative die length in the following sections, given by:-

$$R_L = \frac{L}{R_0} \qquad (6.28)$$

6.5.5 *Comparison with the Straightly Converging Die*

Using the above procedure, the power consumed due to plastic deformation (W_i) and die surface friction (W_s) are computed for the streamlined die as shown in Fig. 6.9 together with the total power consumption. The components of power consumed for the plastic deformation (W_i), velocity discontinuities at the entry (W_e) and the exit (W_f) boundaries, and die surface friction (W_s) are also demonstrated in Fig. 6.9. These power components were computed by the previous solution by Gunasekera and Hoshino, for the same extruding conditions as for the streamlined die. These figures explain the contribution as those for the streamlined die and the contribution of each power component to the total extrusion power.

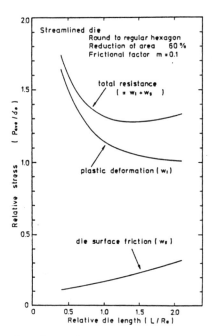

Fig. 6.9 Contribution of power components to the total extrusion power consumed inside the streamlined die

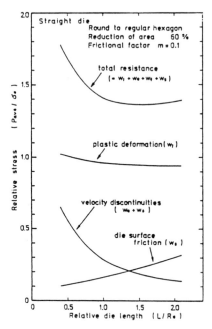

Fig. 6.10 Contribution of power components to the total extrusion power consumed inside the straightly converging die

In the case of extrusion through the streamlined die, the comparison with the total power component due to plastic deformation is dominant, in particular for the shorter length of die. This power, due to plastic deformation, decreases drastically with increase of the die length. This change is attributed to the change of the flow direction inside the plastically deforming 'zone. In contrast, for the straightly converging die, the power component (W_i) remains almost stable at least in the region analyzed here. However, the effects of velocity discontinuities are quite appreciable.

From Fig. 6.10, it is observable that the optimal die length, which requires the minimal total power, is primarily determined by the power components due to velocity discontinuities (W_e, W_f) and die surface friction (W_s).

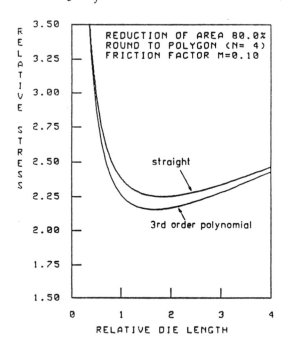

Fig. 6.11 Effect of die profile on the extrusion stresses for square sections

Comparing the streamlined die with the straightly converging die, it is noted that the magnitude of the power component, W_i of the straightly converging die is smaller than that of the streamlined die for the same extruding conditions. However, with regard to the total power, the streamlined die always requires less power as presented in Fig. 6.11. This figure shows the effect of the die profile upon the forming stresses in extrusion. It is clear, in the figure, that the streamlined die defined by cubic curves is superior to the die defined by straight streamlines in terms of the forming stress. The optimal die length of the streamlined die is shorter than that of the straightly converging die. These conclusions have also been verified by experiments performed on lead specimens at room temperature. Details of the experimental work on various die configurations will be reported in subsequent publications.

6.5.6 *Application to Regular Polygonal Sections*

The effect of die surface friction on the relative extrusion stresses required to extrude billets to a square product ($N=4$) are presented in Figs. 6.12 and 6.13 with respect to the relative die length and the reduction of area respectively.

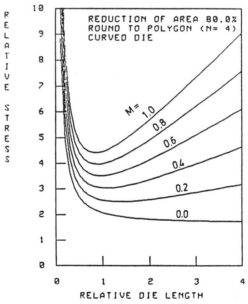

Fig. 6.12 Effect of friction on the extrusion stresses for square section with the die length

The optimal die length which produces the minimal extrusion stress decreases with the increase of friction, and the relative extrusion stress increases with the increase of the reduction of area. Also, the effect of product shape of polygon on the relative extrusion is shown in Fig. 6.14, in which $N = 0$ indicates that the die geometry is an axisymmetrical one.

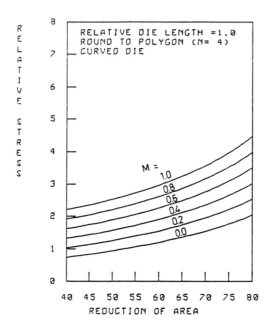

Fig. 6.13 Effect of friction on the extrusion stress for square
section with the reduction of area

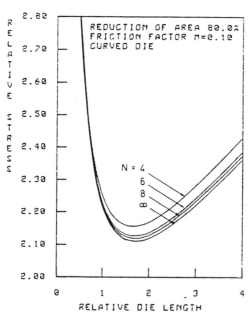

Fig. 6.14 Effect of shape of polygon on the extrusion stress
with the die length

6.6 Application of Finite Element Methods

With the development of better computers, closed-form solutions can be avoided and the use of numerical techniques for the analysis of metal forming processes can be introduced, and the "finite element methods" (FEM), originally devised for structures, is now applied to plastically deformed continuum.

The finite element method is a numerical procedure for obtaining solutions to many of the problems encountered in engineering analysis, and can now be applied to plastic deformation problems, such as forging, extrusion, and rolling. FEM uses continuum elements to obtain solution to heat transfer, fluid mechanics and solid mechanics problems, by approximating values of the desired parameters at specific points called nodes. The finite element method does not give closed-form solutions therefore having the capability to: obtain accurate solutions; provide detailed deformation mechanics; analyse work-hardening material behaviour; and allows interfacial friction constraints to be treated, although with some difficulty.

For the solution of the metal forming problem two approaches can generally be employed. The first is the usual elastic-plastic approach where the material is treated as elastic-plastic. A good example of a computer software package utilizing this approach is NIKE2D developed by JOHN HALLQUIST[37] at the Lawrence Livermore Labs., USA. NIKE2D is an implicit, static and dynamic, finite defromation, finite element computer program for axisymmetric, plane strain and plane stress problems in solid mechanics.

The second is the "rigid-plastic finite element method" developed by Lee and Kobayashi which permitted large increments of deformation, therefore reducing computation time.[38]

An advanced finite element based program ALPID (Analysis of Large Plastic Incremental Deformation), Developed at the Battelle Memorial Institute based on rigid-plasticity under U.S. Air Force Sponsorship was specifically designed for the simulation of plastic deformation involving large incremental plastic strains, to find 2-dimensional metal flow solutions for arbitrary die surfaces in metal forming processes. ALPID provides vital information, including process variables such as strain, strain-rate, stress, and temperature distributions. This information allows the determination of:-

1)   Whether or not the part can be formed without internal and external defects, and

2)   The distribution of local material properties and microstructure at different regions in the formed part.

Although a 3-dimensional version of ALPID and a Turbo ALPID have been developed they are not yet available to the general public, therefore the state-of-the-art in plastic deformation simulation during metal forming processes is the ALPID system.[39]

ALPID simulations were performed for a number of cases of extrusion by OH[40]. Results of one such simulation using a streamlined die are given below:

Die shape	Streamlined Die
Billet Diameter	1 inch
Product Diameter	0.5 inch
Extrusion Ratio	4
Die Length	1 inch
Friction Factor	0.3

Simulations were carried out upto 70 time increments. The original FEM mesh and the grid distortions at 35th and 70th time steps are shown in Figure 6.15. Figures 6.16, 6.17 and 6.18 show the distribution of effective stress, effective strain and effective strain rate sensitivity at the final stage of the extrusion (i.e. 70th step). OH[40] compared his FEM results with experimental grid distortion using split billets and found them to be in very good agreement.

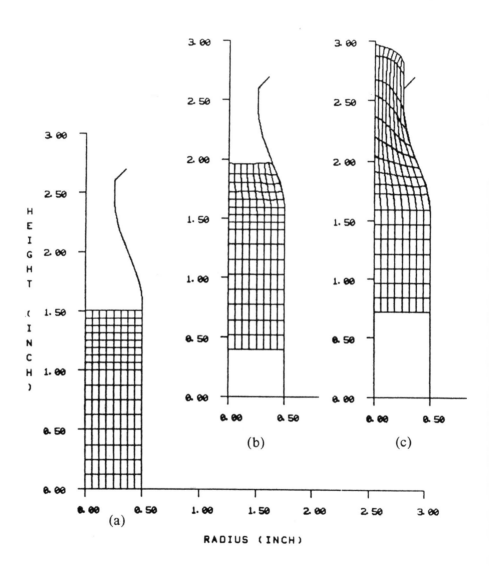

Fig. 6.15 Grid distortion - streamlined die[40]
(a) Initial Grid (step 0), (b) step 35, (c) step 70

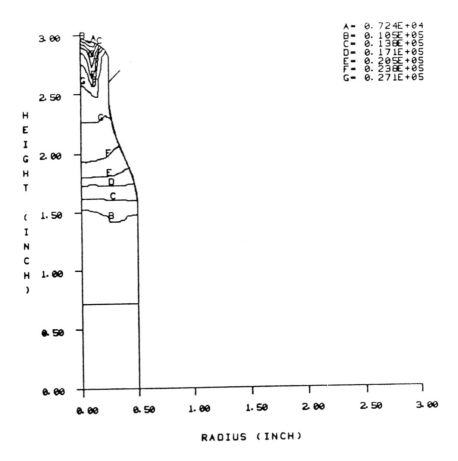

Fig. 6.16 Streamlined die. Effective stress (psi) (Step 70)[40]

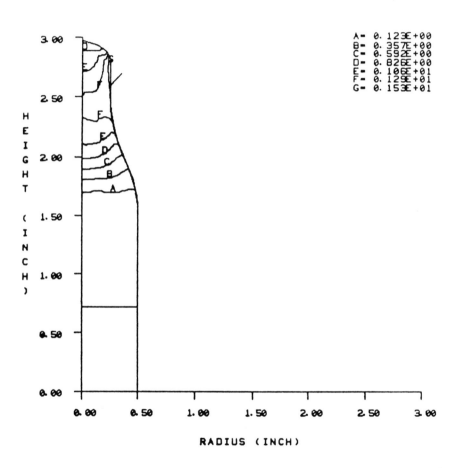

Fig. 6.17 Streamlined die. Effective strain (Step 70)[40]

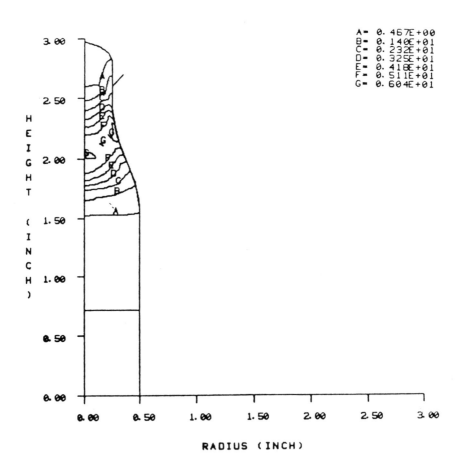

Fig. 6.18 Streamlined die. Effective strain-rate $(1/\text{sec})^{40}$
(Step 70)

REFERENCES

(1) SIEBEL, E., and FANGMEIER, E., "Researches in Power Consumption in the Extrusion and Punching of Metals", *Mitt, K. W. Inst. Eisenfierschung* 1931, **13**, 29-43.

(2) SIEBEL, E., "The Plastic Forming of Metals", Translated by J. H. Hitchcock, Reprinted from *Steel* Oct. 16, 1933, 49-54.

(3) HILL, R., "A Theoretical Analysis of the Stresses and Strains in Extrusion and Piercing", *J. Iron Steel Institute,* 1948, **158**, 177-185.

(4) PRAGER, W. and HODGE, P.G., Jr. *Theory of Perfectly Plastic Solids, Chapter 6.* Wiley, New York, 1951.

(5) GREEN, A.P., "On Unsymmetrical Extrusion in Plane Strain", *J. Mech. Phys. Solids* 1955, **3**, 189.

(6) BISHOP, J.F.W., "The Theory of Extrusion", *Metallurgical Reviews* 1957, **2**, 361-390.

(7) JOHNSON, W., "Extrusion Through Wedge Shaped Dies", *J. Mech. Phys. Solids* 1957, **3**, 218.

(8) KUDO, H., "An Upper Bound Approach to Plane Strain Forging and Extrusion", *Int. J. Mech. Sci.* 1960, **1**, 57-83.

(9) HOFFMAN, O., and SACHS, G., *Introduction to the Theory of Plasticity for Engineers*, pp.163-213. McGraw-Hill, New York, 1953.

(10) GUNASEKERA, J.S. and HOSHINO, S., "Analysis of Extrusion of Drawing of Polygonal Sections Through Strictly Converging Dies", *A.S.M.E. Publication* 1982, **104**, 38-45.

(11) HILL, R., LEE, E.H. and TUPPER, S.J., "A Method of Numerical Analysis of Plastic Flow in Plane Strain and its Application to the Compression of a Ductile Material Between Rough Plates", *Trans. A.S.M.E.* 1951, **73**, 46-52.

(12) GREEN, A.P., "The Theoretical Investigation of The Compression of a Ductile Material Between Smooth Flat Dies", *Phil. Mag.* 1951, **42**, 900.

(13) ALEXANDER, J.M., "The Effect of Coulomb Friction in the Plane Strain Compression of a Plastic-Rigid Material", *J. Mech. Phys. Solids* 1955, **3**, 233-245.

(14) BISHOP, J.F.W., "On The Effect of Friction on Compression and Indentation Between Flat Dies", *J. Mech. Phys. Solids.* 1958, **6**, 132-144.

(15) SIEBEL, E., "*T*he Plastic Forming of Metals", Translated by J. H. Hitchcock, Reprinted from Steel Oct. 16 1933, 20-22.

(16) NADAI, A., "The Forces Required for Rolling Steel Strip Under Tension", *Trans. A.S.M.E., J. App. Mech.* 1939, **6:61**, A-54.

(17) SCHROEDER, W. and WEBSTER, A.W., "Press Forging Thin Sections: Effect of Friction, Area, and Thickness on Pressure Required", *Trans. A.S.M.E., J. App. Mech.* 1949, **16:71**, 289-294.

(18) KOBAYASHI, S., HERZOG, R., LAPSLEY, J.T. and THOMSEN, E.G., "Theory and Experiment of Press Forging Axisymmetric Parts of Aluminum and Lead", *Trans. A.S.M.E., Series B*, 1959, **81**, 228-238.

(19) THOMSEN, E.G., YANG, C.T. and KOBAYASHI, S. *Mechanics of Plastics Deformation in Metal Processing*, pp. 201-214. MacMillan, New York, 1965.

(20) HAAR, A., AND VON KARMAN, T., "Zur Theorie der Spannungszustande in Plastischen und Sandartigen Medien", Nachr. Koniglichen Ges. Wiss. Gottingen, Math. Phys. Kl., 1909, pp. 204.

(21) HILL, R., "The Mathematical Theory of Plasticity", Clarendon Press Oxford, England, 1950.

(22) GUNASEKERA, J.S. and HOSHINO, S., "Analysis of Extrusion or Drawing of Polygonal Sections Through Straightly Converging Dies", *J. Eng. for Ind., Trans. A.S.M.E.* 1982, 104(1) 38-45.

(23) RICHMOND, O. and DEVENPECK, M.L., "A Die Profile for Maximum Efficiency in Strip Drawing", *Proc. 4th U.S. Nat. Congress of App. Mech.* 1962, 2, 1053-1057.

(24) DEVENPECK, M.L. and RICHMOND, O., "Strip Drawing Experiments with a Sigmoidal Die Profile", *J. Eng. for Ind., Trans. A.S.M.E.* 1965, 87(4), 425-428.

(25) HILL, R., "A Remark on Diagonal Streaming in Plane Plastic Strain", *J. Mech. Phys. Solids* 1966, **14**, 245-248.

(26) RICHMOND, O. and MORRISON, H.L., "Streamlined Wire Drawing Dies of Minimum Length", *J. Mech. Phys. Solids* 1967, **15**, 195-200.

(27) DEVENPECK, M.L., *Experimental Evaluation of Theoretically Ideal Drawing Dies*, pp. 215-234. Plenum Press, New York-London, 1971.

(28) NAGPAL, V. and ALTAN, T., "Analysis of the Three-Dimensional Metal Flow in Extrusion of Shapes with the Use of Dual Stream Functions", *Proc. 3rd N.A.M.R.C., Pittsburgh, PA.* 1975, pp. 26-40.

(29) NAGPAL, V., "On the Solution of Three–Dimensional Metal–Forming Processes", *J. Eng. for Ind., Trans. A.S.M.E.* 1977, 99(3), 624-629.

(30) YANG, D.Y. and LEE, C.H., "Analysis of Three–Dimensional Extrusion of Sections Through Curved Dies by Conformal Transformation", *Int. J. Mech. Sci.* 1978a, 20, 541-552.

(31) YANG, D.Y., KIM, M.U. and LEE, C.H., "An Analysis for Extrusion of Helical Shapes from Round Billets", *Int. J. Mech. Sci.* 1978b, 20, 695–705.

(32) HOSHINO, S., "Extrusion of Non-Axisymmetric Sections through Converging Dies", *Ph.D. Thesis,* Monash University, Australia, 1981.

(33) CHEN, C.T. and LING, F.F., "Upper–Bound Solutions to Axisymmetric Extrusion Problems", *Int. J. Mech. Sci.* 1968, 10, 863-879.

(34) FRISCH, J. and MATA-PIETRI, E., "Experiments and Upper Bound Solution in Axisymmetric Extrusion", *Proc.18th Int.M.T.D.R.Conf.* pp.55-60. Imperial College, London, 1977.

(35) MATA-PIETRI, E. and FRISCH, J., "Metal Flow Through Various Mathematically Contoured Extrusion Dies", *Proc. 5th N.A.M.R.C.* 1977.

(36) AVITZUR, B., *Metal Forming: Processes and Analyses.* McGraw-Hill, New York, 1968.

(37) HALLQUIST, J.O., "NIKE2D: An Implicit Finite Deformation Finite Element Code for Analyzing The Static and Dynamic Response of Two-Dimensional Solids", Univ. of California, Lawrence Livermore National Labs., *Rept UCRL-52678*, March 1979.

(38) LEE, C.H. and KOBAYASHI, S. "New Solutions to Rigid-Plastic Deformation Problems using a Matrix Method", Trans. ASME, J. of Eng. for Ind. 1973, pp. 95.

(39) ALPID System User's Manual, Version 2.0, Battelle, Columbus Division, Columbus, Ohio, November 1985.

(40) OH, Y.S., "Extrusion of Axisymmetric Sections through Streamlined and Conical Dies", *M.S. Thesis*, Ohio University, Athens, August 1987.

Chapter 7

COMPUTER AIDED MANUFACTURE OF COMPLEX DIES

7.1 Introduction

The problem of shape representation is of vital importance in CAD/CAM, particularly for shapes such as ship hulls, aircraft exterior parts, forging, extrusion and moulding dies etc. where the geometry may not be defined analytically. The geometry and shape of parts (and surfaces of parts) become the central data base within a CAD/CAM system which interconnects with other functions such as design, analysis, drafting and manufacturing. The advent of interactive computing, graphics facilities and NC (numerically controlled) machines has made it possible to design and manufacture geometrically complex shapes with considerable ease.

Since the pioneering work on three-dimensional curved surfaces representation by COONS[1], FERGUSON[2], BEZIER[3,4] and many others, there now exist software packages which are capable of representing curved engineering surfaces using the computer. Work done by NAGPAL *et al.*[5] at Battelle Columbus Labs. on extrusion and forging dies, KNIGHT *et al.*[6] at Oxford University, U.K., GUNASEKERA and HOSHINO[7], and JAYASURIYA[8], at Monash University, Australia, KAVULASKAS[9] at the Wright-Patterson Air Force Base, and MEHTA[10] at Ohio University is all noteworthy in the metal working area. As for plastics injection moulding dies – WANG *et al.*[11] at Cornell University and MEHTA and COLLIER[12,13] at Ohio Uiversity for shaped extrusion dies, have made valuable contributions. Work done by DAVIES and SIAUW[14] (CSIRO, Australia) in the CAD/CAM of die-casting dies is also noteworthy. Commercial software packages such as MOLDFLOW, STREAM, SHAPE and CUTTER are now available.

7.2 Sculptured Surfaces

Two types of surface are encountered in numerical control (NC) applications. The first is a surface that can be defined analytically (i.e. by a single equation – for example a plane or a cylinder). The second is a surface described by a coarse grid of points in space and the use of surface fitting algorithms which is termed a 'sculptured surface'. The former is relatively simple and easy to use. For example in the APT language (Automatically Programmed Tools is probably the most comprehensive and best known of all NC language processors.), planes and cylinders can be defined in many ways, for example:

plane = PLANE/PARLEL, plane, ZLARGE, d

or a circle as:
circle = CIRCLE/point, point, point
for a circle passing through three points.

Unlike analytic surfaces, the sculptured surface cannot be defined by a single mathematical relationship. Hence the need to develop methods for defining such surfaces in a manner suitable for NC applications. Two basic methods have been developed in the past. Early investigators used 'Multivariable curve interpolation' (FERGUSON[2]) methods while the more recent investigators have used 'parametric patches' (COONS[1]) to describe sculptured surfaces.

7.3 Developments of APT Leading to Sculptured Surfaces

The following is a summary of the developments of different geometric types, (HINDS[15]).

a)   Conventional unbounded planes, cones, cylinders and other analytical surfaces.
b)   Tabulated cylinders (TAB CYL) which are surfaces created by use of a splining algorithm to create a space curve through the desired set of points.
c)   Ruled surface (RLD SRF). This is the most sophisticated surface that occurs within standard APT, being a surface composed of straight line rulings between two tabulated cylinders or other curves.
d)   FMILL/APTLOFT (developed by Ferguson at Boeing and Coons at M.I.T.) − FMILL provides a sculptured surface capacity using a coarse mesh of points as input. It generates surface patches and from these produces a dense mesh of points and surface normals. These are then fed to an APT processor with the APTLOFT modification and this generates the final cutter path. This development became the predecessor of sculptured surfaces. It does

however impose limitations on the user's ability to use the sculptured surface in a truly general manner.

e) Parametric Surfaces in APTIV - was very effective but required skilled scientific programmers to implement its use.

f) Sculptured Surface enhancements to APTIV as developed by CAM-I and others allow the sculptured surfaces to be used in a completely general way. In APT terminology the sculptured surface can be used as a drive part or check surface with a large range of cutter geometries provided for by APT.

7.4 Sculptured Geometry

Surfaces are collections of bounded parametric patches, each expressed in terms of known points, vectors, and curves together with blending and interpolation formulas. The Coons' parametric patch is a unit square twisted and distorted in space. The common bi-cubic patch satisfies slope continuity at the edges in addition to positional continuity. It is completely defined by the four corner points, eight tangent vectors (in two directions) and four twist vectors. The mathematics of the bi-cubic patch is dealt with in numerous publications (FORREST[16]). The less commonly used 'bi-quintic' patch satisfies the curvature continuity at the boundaries of the adjacent patches in addition to the slope and positional continuities (MUNCHMEYER[17]).

7.5 SSX8

CAM-I (Computer Aided Manufacturing - International, Arlington, Texas, U.S.A.) has been involved in the development of sculptured surface software for some time. Early contracts were given to IITRI (Illinois Institute of Technology - Research Institute) and the more recent ones to NIU (Northern Illinois University). SSX8 is the latest version of this software development. Monash University, Australia, obtained this package in 1979 and has been testing and using it in collaboration with ACI Computer Services.

One of the major problems with this system is that it is so powerful in terms of defining 'any' surface - that the system can be used to define surfaces which cannot even be machined! APT sculptured surfaces can be examined inter-actively using CASPA (Computer-Aided Sculptured Pre-APT

System) – developed by Hinds and Kuan at NIU . CASPA is a preprocessor and combines sculptured geometry with a graphics processor. CASPA could be used in both design and manufacturing applications.

7.6 Application of Sculptured Surface Software to Extrusion Dies

The computer aided design of streamlined extrusion dies is well documented (GUNASEKERA[18], GUNASEKERA and HOSHINO[19]) (see Chapter 5). The geometry of the die is defined by the entry section (which is usually circular), the exit section (product sectional shape) and a series of splines connecting the entry and exit sections. Fig. 7.1 shows the geometry of a die having a circular entry shape and a square exit shape. Figure 7.2 shows a modified die with rounded corners.

HOSHINO and GUNASEKERA[20] used the SSX8 package to model these shapes and produce NC tapes via the APT system. The die with rounded corners did not pose any problems for SSX8 or APT and the entire die could be modelled as one surface. Problems were encountered with the original die which had a sharp-cornered square for its exit shape. Similar error messages showed up for the die which had a regular hexagon for its exit shape. These were due to the discontinuity imposed in the surface by the sharp corners. Ball end milling cutters were used in all cases. The essential elements of the typical SSX8 program are shown in the Appendix. The computer output from this program will include a mesh pattern of points and normals at those points and other useful information such as the total area of the surface and the critical curvatures.

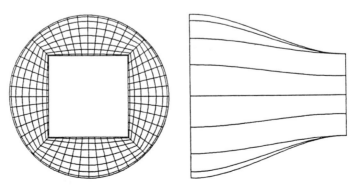

Fig.7.1 Extrusion die geometry (round to square)

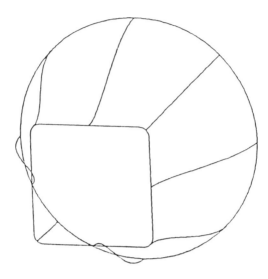

Fig. 7.2 Round to square with rounded corners

7.7 Methods of Overcoming the Problem of Sharp Corners

Three approaches were considered for a solution to the problem of sharp corners. The first approach was to write a new computer program which would generate NC commands for the manufacture of this particular shape (i.e extrusion dies), using a simple flat-ended cutter and cut vectors short enough to maintain a close tolerance. This method is elaborated in detail in the following sections.

The other two approaches have not been tried up to this stage — but will be briefly explained here for the benefit of future users. The SSX8 scupltured surface software used does not allow the inclusion of sharp discontinuities because it is designed to fair curves. It is possible to deal with the sharp corners treating the die (with the square exit shape) to consist of a number of sub-surfaces, each of which can be easily defined through SSX8, with the check surfaces defined through the discontinuities. SSX8 is a powerful tool and it is up to the imagination of the user to devise methods for re-defining the same problem in different ways.

Another approach for a solution to this 'sharp corner' problem may be to use multiple vertices in B-splines — as described by VEENMAN[21] of Shape Data Ltd. The B-spline technique was first developed in France by Bezier. He pioneered a new interactive technique whereby the shape of a curve was defined by the shape of an associated polygon. The application of B-splines improved the user's control over the shape of the curve or surface and provided a sound mathematical foundation to the method.

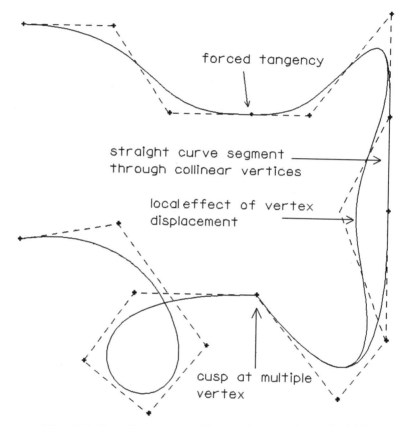

Fig. 7.3 B-spline curve illustrating various facilities
(after VEENMAN[21])

Fig. 7.3 illustrates the various facilities available with B-splines. The important facility from the viewpoint of the present problem is its ability to form a cusp at the multiple vertex as shown in Fig. 7.3.

7.8 Profile of the Extrusion Dies

The details of the extrusion die to be manufactured are tabulated in Table 7.1. As regular hexagonal sections are to be extruded from round bar stocks in the final extrusion trials, the die entry has a circular section and the exit shape is a regular hexagon. Reduction of area is kept constant at 60 per cent and four different die-lengths are used in the present investigation. The die-length indicates the distance between entry and exit sections.

TABLE 7.1 *Geometry of extrusion dies*

Entry shape	Round (radius: 10 mm
Exit shape	Regular hexagon
Reduction of area	60 per cent
Die profile	Streamlined die (smooth entry and exit)
Length of die	5, 10, 15, 20 (mm)
Length of die land	5 mm

Since one of the main objectives of the present investigation is to manufacture the extrusion die which produces a smooth material flow during the deformation process, the entry section of the die should be connected with the exit by an envelope of smooth streamlines. For this purpose third order polynomial curves having (entry and exit) tangents parallel to the longitudinal axis are chosen. As a result of this the required shape of the extrusion die becomes complex and necessitates the use of an NC (numerical control) milling machine for its machining. Direct machining of the cavity is difficult as the final hexagonal section has sharp corners. It is therefore necessary to shape up an electrode having an almost identical profile to the die cavity for subsequent electro-discharge machining.

7.9 Determination of the Tool Path for NC Milling

As mentioned earlier, instead of using existing sculptured software packages which normally require a mainframe computer (such as an IBM computer for SSX8), HOSHINO and GUNASEKERA[20] decided to develop a new method to convert geometrical data of the extrusion die surface into the path

of tool motion using a minicomputer.   The effort to produce
complex geometries using a minicomputer is of interest since
some companies dealing with the manufacture of engineering
parts have (or have access to) minicomputers.

Machining electrodes by ball-end milling cutter introduces
an awkward 3-D geometrical problem when determining the
position of the cutter (although it produces a surface with
minimal machining marks).   Therefore, for brevity of the
analysis, a flat-ended cutter is used.   The employment of a
flat-ended milling cutter rotating around the longitudinal axis
of the electrode can simplify the geometry problem.   (The use
of the flat-ended cutter, however, leaves steps on the
electrode necessitating many more cuts to achieve an
acceptable finish for hand polishing.)   The correlation between
the electrode surface to be machined and the locus of the
flat-ended cutter is shown in Fig. 7.4.

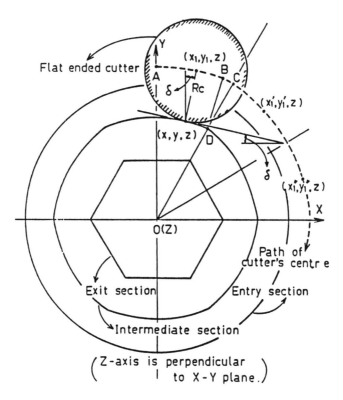

Fig.7.4 Geometry of the electrode and the cutter

The equation of the streamlines along the electrode
surface in a cartesian coordinate system is formulated as:

$$x = R_0 \sin \varphi + (ac\varphi - R_0 \sin \varphi).f(z)$$

$$y = R_0 \cos \varphi + (a - R_0 \cos \varphi).f(z) \qquad (7.1)$$

$$z = z$$

where:

$$f(z) = 3\left[\frac{z}{L}\right]^2 - 2\left[\frac{z}{L}\right]^3 \qquad\qquad c = \frac{6}{\pi} \tan \left[\frac{\pi}{6}\right]$$

In those equations, R_0 is the radius of the circular entry section, a is a half side length of the hexagonal section, and φ is an angle between the symmetrical plane and the stream surface at the entry section. Details relevant to Equation 7.1 are given by HOSHINO and GUNASEKERA[20]. Angle φ at the point (x,y,z) on the contour of the intermediate cross section (in Fig. 7.4) is expressed by using Equation 7.1 as follows:

$$\tan \delta = - \frac{\partial y}{\partial x} = - \frac{\partial y}{\partial \varphi} \cdot \frac{\partial \varphi}{\partial x}$$

$$= \frac{R_0[1 - f(z)] \sin \varphi}{R_0[1 - f(z)] \cos \varphi + ac\, f(z)} \qquad (7.2)$$

Knowing angle φ and the radius of the cutter (R_c), the corresponding coordinate on the locus of cutter (x_1,y_1,z) which is normal to the tangent of the contour is easily found. Due to symmetry in shape, the calculation of coordinates for the cutter motion is required only for the locus between points A and B. The locus between points B and C is obtained by simply rotating the cutter around point D maintaining the distance of R_c, as the contour of the intermediate cross-section is discontinuous at point D. Symmetrically mirrored coordinates (x_1',y_1',z) and (x_1'',y_1'',z) are determined as:

$$x_1' = y_1 \cos(\pi/6) - x_1 \sin(\pi/6)$$

$$y_1' = y_1 \sin(\pi/6) + x_1 \cos(\pi/6)$$

$$x_1'' = y_1 \cos(\pi/6) + x_1 \sin(\pi/6) \qquad (7.3)$$

$$y_1'' = y_1 \sin(\pi/6) - x_1 \cos(\pi/6)$$

The complete locus of one cut along the fixed x-y plane can be obtained by interchanging positive and negative signs of coordinates or x and y coordinates determined through Equations 7.1, 7.2 and 7.3. Shifting the cutter along the longitudinal axis with sequentially incremental depth, produces the entire electrode.

7.10 Generation of NC Tapes and the Shape of Machined Electrodes

The procedure to generate NC tapes from the raw data of surface or tool path coordinates is illustrated in Fig. 7.5. Machine processor programming is required to combine the coordinates of the machined surface or the cutter's locus with the actual cutter's motion for milling, and to convert them to NC tape. This postprocessor is dependent upon the type of NC machine to be used. These programs have been developed for several types of NC milling machines at "Diecraft Australia." Using one of the programs and a DIGITAL PDP-11, computer NC tapes were generated for the milling machine (MAKINO).

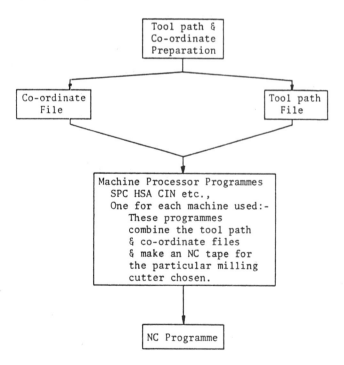

Fig. 7.5 Schematic of NC tape generation

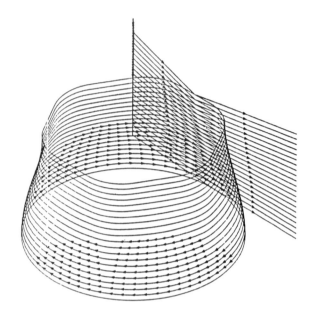

Fig. 7.6 Tool path

Before punching the tapes, the tool path was plotted on the plotting facility as shown in Fig. 7.6.   Each path of the tool comprises 121 points of coordinates to achieve the required accuracy.

(a)   (b)

Fig. 7.7 NC machined electrodes (a) 5 mm length,
(b) 20 mm length

Fig. 7.7 shows the prototype of machined electrodes for 5 mm and 20 mm length of dies, respectively.   The material used for electrodes is commercially pure copper.   It is found that the optimal incremental depth for the sequential step in the direction of longitudinal axis is 0.25 mm in order to avoid unnecessary distortion of the profile during handfiling. Therefore, this value was used for all different lengths of the dies.   In consequence the required length of NC tapes becomes 108 m (360 ft.) for a 5 mm length of die, and 213 m (709 ft) for a 20 mm length of die.

7.11 Extrusion Dies and the Accuracy of Their Shape

An extrusion die HOSHINO and GUNASEKERA[20] manufactured using this method and a partially extruded product are shown in Fig. 7.8.   These extrusion dies were made of AIRDIE 150 alloy which were heat-treated to obtain the specified hardness (Rockwell C scale 60 to 62) prior to electro-discharge machining (EDM).   Wear compensation of the electrode has been taken into account in order to produce an accurate shape with a specified tolerance.

After EDM the extrusion die cavities were highly polished (CLA = 0.04 μm approximately).   The accuracy of the extrusion die cavities were checked after the first commercially pure lead billets were extruded by projecting the billets onto the profile projector (NIKON, Model V-16).   Results are shown in Fig. 7.9.   It has been observed that the final shape of any extrusion die manufactured using the method explained here is very accurate.

Fig. 7.8 Extrusion die and product

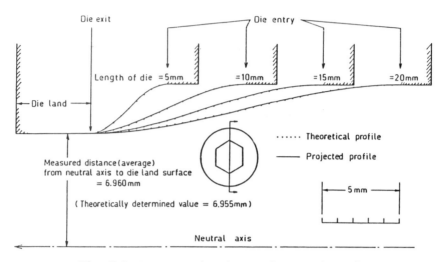

Fig. 7.9 Accuracy in shape of extrusion die

7.12 Use of a Turnkey CAD/CAM System for the Manufacture of Dies

This approach is perhaps the easiest if a turnkey CAD/CAM system is readily available. The die design geometry can be transferred to the CAD/CAM system via a suitable interface and the CL field generated using the CAD/CAM system.

7.13 'CUTTER' - An Alternative Approach to CAM of Dies

JAYASURIYA and GUNASEKERA[8] developed a soft-ware package for the CAM of dies. This package is complimentary to the die design package STREAM, and the product geometry is stored in a common data file for use by both programs.

Two major constraints were set at the beginning of this investigation in order to produce an end product which would be readily adoptable for industrial use:

i)   The design of algorithms and the software must be such that the resulting package should be capable of being implemented on a microcomputer as well as on a mini.

ii)   The N.C. machining centre to be utilized requires only 3 fully programmable axes.

As a consequence of restriction (ii), a ball-nose cutter must be utilized as the metal removing tool. These are relatively cheap and are commonly used in a tool-making environment. The inefficiency of these cutters as metal removing tools can be tolerated in a low volume tool making environment.

7.14 N.C. Machining of the Electrodes

The electrode can be machined in either of the positions shown in Fig. 7.10. In Fig. 7.10(a), the cutter will be driven in the yz-plane and in Fig. 7.10(b), it will be driven in the xz plane with indexing along the y-axis. The former position has clear advantages:

a)   Long series cutters are not required even for large work-pieces. This improves the rigidity of the cutter, reducing chatter and vibration effects, resulting in a better surface finish.

b)   The workpiece can be held rigidly between centres during the machining process increasing the accuracy of the operation.

Consequently the electrode is to be machined in the position shown in Fig. 7.10(a)

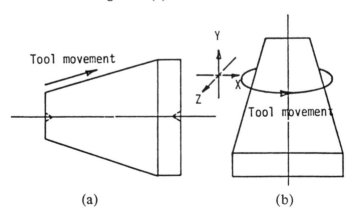

(a)   (b)

Fig. 7.10 Suitable work piece orientations for machining
on a vertical milling machine

The requirements in producing cutter paths to drive an NC cutting tool can be outlined as follows:

a)   The tool movement must result in a surface that is within:

   i)   tolerance along the cutter paths (longitudinal tolerance)
   ii)   tolerance occurring radially on the perimeter of the billet end of the electrode (scallop tolerance).

b)   Determination of the coordinates of the cutter centre with appropriate corrections made for the cutter offset.
c)   Possible interference between the tool and the workpiece must be removed.

Due to the restriction of using a 3-axis machine, a dividing head must be utilized for rotation of the workpiece to enable the cutter to gain access to the complete workpiece. Therefore the workpiece is divided (interactively by the user) into regions and these are individually considered for analysis. As an example consider Fig. 7.11.

In general, any shape can be machined utilizing this method. The manual operation of the dividing head can be avoided by having a 4th axis which can be programmed to index through predefined angles. (Most 3-axis machine controllers can be easily extended to cover a fourth programmable axis.)

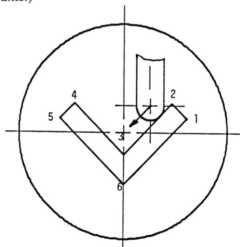

Nodes 1, 2, 3, 4, and 5 constitute region 1
and Nodes 5, 6, and 1 constitute region 2.

Fig. 7.11 Division of the workpiece into regions
to facilitate the machining operation

7.15 Longitudinal Tolerance

During the machining process, the cutter movement will be linear between discrete points identified along the cutter paths. This results in a deviation of the cut surface from that desired (illustrated in Fig. 7.12).

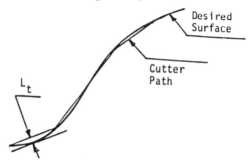

Fig. 7.12 Illustration of the longitudinal tolerance

For the accuracies required in the manufacture of streamlined extrusion dies, it is adequate to evaluate the deviation between the two surfaces, at the mid-point of each segment. This is performed for each segment along each one of the cutter paths. The maximum value of the longitudinal tolerance L_t is determined and compared against the user-entered longitudinal tolerance. The number of nodes is adjusted until the maximum L_t is less than the entered tolerance. Clearly the number of nodes required will increase with finer tolerances. An example is given in Appendix A.

7.16 Scallop Tolerance

During the machining operation, the cutter is required to traverse the workpiece along the z-axis, making several passes along a predefined direction. The coarseness of these passes is governed by the acceptable scallop height S_t between two consecutive cutter paths. This is illustrated in Fig. 7.13. Clearly, it is advantageous to have a small value for S_t, in order to facilitate subsequent finishing operations. The smaller the S_t, the larger the number of passes required. One way of avoiding this problem would be to use a larger diameter cutter. However, the product geometry often restricts the size of the cutter permitted to be used on a given job. Consider the billet end of the workpiece (see Fig. 7.13). It is possible to establish a simple geometric relationship between various variables and S_t.

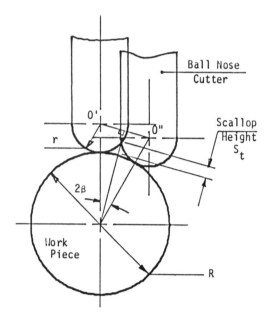

Fig 7.13 Geometric relationship between the tool,
electrode and scallop height

$$\cos \beta = \frac{1}{2}\left[\frac{(R+S_t)^2+R(R+2r)}{(R+S_t).(R+r)}\right] \qquad (7.4)$$

Given R, r and S_t, Equation 7.4 can be solved for β and, consequently, the number of passes required for each region can be established. Addition of these passes gives the total number of passes required for the operation. Note that this calculation reflects the worst case since, as the electrode converges toward the product the surface finish will be better than that produced at the billet end to the specified scallop tolerance. An example of this calculation is given in Appendix A.

It must be noted that the initial value for β, obtained through the solution of Equation 7.4, may not result in an integer number of tool passes within the region currently under analysis. Thus the calculated number of tool passes is rounded up to the closest integer number. Knowing the included angle of a region and the number of passes for the region, a new value for β can be calculated. Then Equation 7.5 below is solved for the new value of S_t, which will be the scallop dimension produced on the workpiece. (the resulting value of S_t will be smaller than the user-entered value thus ensuring no loss in the accuracy).

$$S_t^2 + AS_t + B = 0 \qquad\qquad (7.5)$$

where: $A = 2[R - (R+r) \cos \beta]$

$B = [R^2 + R(R+2r) - 2R(R+r) \cos \beta]$

The solution of the quadratic Equation 7.5 is best performed numerically by the use of "Newton's Method" since a good approximation to the root S_t is known beforehand.

7.17 Cutter Offset

The cutter must be accurately offset from the final surface grid resulting from the tolerance requirements (see Fig. 7.14).

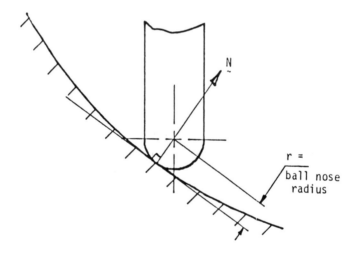

Fig. 7.14 Correct offset resulting in the accurate positioning of the cutter relative to the work-piece surface

The requirement is to generate a vector normal to the surface, at each of the nodes on the cutter path. The cutter is then offset at a distance r along the normal.

Consider the patch illustrated in Fig. 7.15. Positional vectors at each node, $\underline{A_i}$ and $\underline{B_i}$ ($i = 1$......total nodes) are known. Therefore $\underline{A}$ and $\underline{B}$ are known.

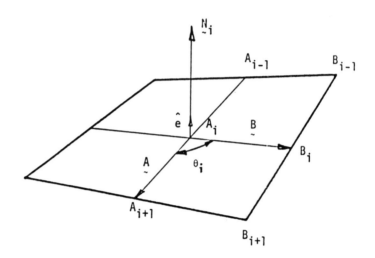

Fig. 7.15 Typical patch on the surface of an electrode

The angle between these two vectors is calculated by taking the inverse cosine of the dot product between $\underline{A}$ and $\underline{B}$, as follows:

$$\theta_i = \cos^{-1} \left[\frac{\underline{A} \cdot \underline{B}}{|A| \; |B|} \right] \tag{7.6}$$

$$N_i = \underline{A} \times \underline{B} \tag{7.7}$$

Normalizing vector $\underline{N_i}$

$$\hat{e}_i = \frac{[\underline{A} \times \underline{B}]}{|A| \; |B| \; \sin \theta_i} \tag{7.8}$$

then: $$\underline{OO'} = \hat{e}_i \times R + \underline{OA_i} \tag{7.9}$$

where: $\underline{OO'}$ = position vector of the cutter centre

and: $\underline{OA_i}$ = position vector of A_i.

Therefore, the components of OO' are known and consequently the $x, y,$ and z coordinates of O' edges are known. Care must be exercised at the edges so that the direction of the normal is not reversed during the vector cross product operation.

7.18 Tool, Work-piece Interference

Interference between the tool and the workpiece can be divided into two categories:

a)   Collision: This occurs when the tool moves to a new cutting location. The solution is two-fold:

   (1)   Through the use of interactive graphics, the user is allowed to divide the workpiece into different regions thus avoiding collision and also optimizing the workpiece orientation for machining position.

   (2)   By defining "clear points" at each end of the cutter path, collision is avoided during the rapid traverse of the tool from the end of one cutter path to the beginning of another (see Appendix A). At present this is edited into the CL File by the user. A facility is being incorporated to allow the user to define these points interactively.

b)   Gouging: This is the more difficult aspect of interference. Consider Fig. 7.11. The analysis for cutter paths in region 1 would be performed in the order 1, 2, 3, 4. However, as the cutter moves near node 3, along face 2-3, it will gouge out material from face 3-4. Likewise as the cutter moves from 3 to 4, it will remove material from face 2-3.

The smallest section of a streamline extrusion die is at the product end. Therefore, gouging will be checked at this end by a suitable algorithm. The CL File must then be edited to remove the undesirable cutter locations. The difficulties lie in developing fool-proof algorithms for the detection of gouging.

Current research efforts are directed towards this problem.

7.19 Cutter Location File (CL File)

The coordinate information produced in Section 7.16 must be further processed to obtain a format acceptable to N.C. machines. Some editing must be performed on this file for the addition of machine-dependent features (typically 15 lines). It is possible to view the cutter paths graphically enabling instant verification of the cutter paths (See Appendix A).

7.20 Applications

The current version of the package is running on a mini-computer VAX-11 which is a 32-bit machine.   At present automatic gouging detection is not available.   The electrodes shown in Appendix A were manufactured using a 'Zenford-Zigler' 3-axes N.C. machine which utilized an ANCA CNC control.   The machine buffer accommodated approximately 300 lines.   Therefore the CL file was divided into blocks of 300 lines and loaded via a DEC PDP 11/23 host computer.   The resulting surface was satisfactory.

A similar CAD/CAM system was modified and adopted by MEHTA and COLLIER[13] to design and manufacture multiple hole dies for fibre spinning, coating, and for profile extrusion of neat and reinforced polymeric materials.   A multiple   die with 37 holes (Fig. 7.16) was designed using this CAD system and manufactured on a Bridgeport 3-axis CNC milling machine (Fig. 7.17).   An alternative approach is to machine one graphite or copper electrode and use this to Electro-Discharge Machine (EDM) (see Fig. 7.18) the die cavities.

The CAD system[10] was also adopted to design hollow dies with shaped mandrel for high pressure co-extrusion of pipes (Fig. 7.19).   The mandrel and cavity are streamlined which significantly reduce extrudate defects on the inner and outer surface of the pipe.   The high pressure co-extrusion die was machined on a Mazak turning centre (Fig. 7.20).

Fig. 7.16 Multiple hole die (37 holes) for fibre coating[13]

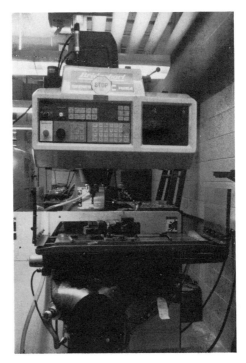

Fig. 7.17 A bridgeport 3-axis CNC/DNC milling machine

Fig. 7.19 High pressure co-extrusion/Die for hollow products
(pipes)[13]

Fig. 7.20 A Mazak turning centre

Fig. 7.18 EASCO EDM (Electro-Discharge Machine)

REFERENCES

(1) COONS, S.A., "Surfaces for Computer–Aided–Design of Space Figures" *M.I.T. ESL 9442–M–139*, 1964.

(2) FERGUSON, J., "Multivariable Curve Interpolation", *J. of Assoc. for Computing Machinery* 11(2), 221–228.

(3) BEZIER, P.E., "Example of an Existing System in the Motor Industry: The Unisurf System" *Proc. Roy. Soc. Lond.* 1971, A.321, 207–218.

(4) BEZIER, P.E., *Numerical Control – Mathematics and Applications*, Wiley, London, 1972.

(5) NAGPAL, V. and ALTAN, T., "Analysis of 3-D Metalflow in Extrusion of Shapes With The Use of Dual Stream Functions", *Proc. of the 3rd North American Metalworking Research Conf.*, Pittsburgh, PA, 1975, pp. 26-40.

(6) BARIANI, P. and KNIGHT, W.A., "Computer-Aided Cold Forging Process Design: A Knowledge-Based System Approach to Forming Sequence Generation", *Annals of the CIRP*, 1988, 37(1), 243.

(7) GUNASEKERA, J.S. and HOSHINO, S., "Analysis of Extrusion or Drawing of Polygonal Sections Through Straightly Converging Dies", *ASME Journal for Ind.*, 1982, 104(1), 38-45.

(8) GUNASEKERA, J.S. and JAYASURIYA, J., "Computer Aided Manufacturing of Streamlined Extrusion Dies", *ASME Intl. Computers in Engineering*, Las Vegas, USA, 1984, 2, 393-400.

(9) KAVULASKAS, R., GUNASEKERA, J.S., GEGEL, H.L., DORAIVELU, S.M., and MALAS, J.C., "Use of CAD/CAM to Manufacture Streamlined Dies for Extrusion of Complex Materials", *Proc. of 11th N.A.M.R.C.*, Wisconsin, May 1983, pp. 252-258.

(10) MEHTA, B.V., "Computer Aided Design of Streamlined Dies", Master's Thesis, Ohio University, Athens, Ohio, USA, March 88.

(11) WANG, K.K., SHEN, S.F., HIEBER, C.A., and COHEN, C., "Recent Findings in Injection Molding Research", *14th Conf. on Production Research and Tech., Conf. Proc. Edited by Prof. S.K. Samantha*, Ann Arbor, MI., Oct 6-9, 1987.

(12) COLLIER, J.R., GUNASEKERA, J.S, and MEHTA, B.V., "CAD/CAM of Streamlined Dies for Polymer Extrusion", *SPE RETEC'87*, Dearborn, MI., Nov. 1987, pp. 146.

(13) MEHTA, B.V. and COLLIER, J.K., "Computer Aided Design/Computer Aided Manufacture of Dies for Polymer Extrusion", *Proc. of the 6th National Conf. of Univ. Programs in Computer Aided Engineering, Design and Manufacture (PGCAEDM'88),* Georgia Institute of Tech., Atalnta, Georgia, July 1988, pp. 193-197.

(14) DAVIS, A.J. and SIAUW, T.H., "Metalflow - A System for The Design and Manufacture of Metal Flow Systems for Dies", *Soc. of Die Casting Engineers 13th Intl. Die Casting Congress and Exposition,* Milwaukee, WI., June 3-6, 1985.

(15) HINDS, J.K., KUAN, L.P., and WARNER, J.C., "CAM–I Sculptured Surfaces User's Course", *CAM–I, Texas TM–77–SS–01* 1977.

(16) FORREST, A.R., "On Coons and other methods for the representation of curved surfaces", *Computer Graphics* 1972, 1, 341–359.

(17) MUNCHMEYER, F., "The Gaussian Curvature of Coons biquintic patches", *A.S.M.E. Int. Comp. Tech. Conf.,* San Fransisco 1980, 383–387.

(18) GUNASEKERA, J.S., "Computer Aided Modelling and Design of Shaped Extrusion Dies", *A.S.M.E. Int. Comp. Tech. Conf.,* San Fransisco 1980, 452–459.

(19) GUNASEKERA, J.S. and HOSHINO, S., "Extrusion of Non–Circular Sections Through Shaped Dies", *CIRP Annals* 1980, 21(1), 141–145.

(20) HOSHINO, S. and GUNASEKERA, J.S., "An Upper Bound Solution for the Extrusion of Square Section from Round Bar Through Converging Dies", *Proc. Int. MTDR* 1980, 21, 97–105.

(21) VEENMAN, P., "Introduction to the use of B–Splines for Describing Curves and Surfaces", *Shape Data Ltd.,* England 1979,1–18.

Chapter 8

FUTURE OF CAD/CAM OF DIES

8.1 Introduction

CAD/CAM are affecting almost every area of engineering. During the last decade or so, progress and advances made in this field have been outstanding. As a result, instead of just using heuristic techniques for die design, designers are now switching over to analytical and process modelling techniques using computers. The outcome of these designs, that is, the optimum solution, is dependent on a number of factors, but depends primarily on the knowledge and experience of the designer. Expert systems, a relatively new field in design and manufacturing, uses this idea of expert knowledge to achieve a workable, economical, and optimum solution of a problem in lesser time. This has become all the more important due to increased competition, greater demand, and varying standards in industry.

This chapter introduces the reader to expert systems, their basic setup, use of expert systems in CAD/CAM of dies, expert systems in present use, and finally, the future of CAD/CAM of dies.

8.2 Introduction to Expert Systems

Expert system is an attempt to capture the expertise and knowledge of a design engineer in a computer program. This computer program exploits the power of existing analytical tools, CAD/CAM techniques for die design, and heuristic rules, to emulate tasks normally done by experts in this field. Expert system is implemented by coalescing Computer Aided Engineering (CAE), Computer Aided Design (CAD), and Computer Aided Manufacturing (CAM) techniques in die design. Although the aforementioned techniques are used separately to achieve a workable solution, nevertheless, there is no tool which connects the three and integrates the manufacturing system spanning the steps from concept formulation to manufacturing.

GUNASEKERA, DORAIVELU, AND RAMANTHAN[1], put forward two methodologies in designing and manufacturing dies.

In the first method, the design of the die is obtained by making use of the CAE systems approach. This approach (GUNASEKERA, GEGEL, MALAS, DORAIVELU, MORGAN, GRIFFIN[2]), integrates dynamic behaviour modelling, geometric modelling, analytical process modelling, CAD/CAM of dies, and process control as illustrated in Fig. 8.1.

- PART DESIGN
- PROCESS ANALYSIS
- DIE DESIGN

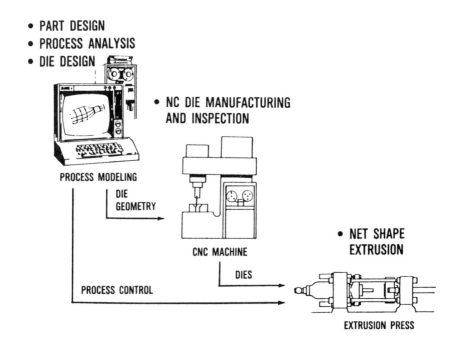

Fig. 8.1 Computer Aided Engineering approach[1]

In the second method, well established empirical rules are used for arriving at an acceptable design alternative. Currently, both procedures follow a trial and error approach to achieve the required goal. Either one used by itself is a time consuming and costly process. The CAE process lacks empirical aids during the selection of an initial design and the experience based method lacks analytical aids for verification of the final design.   The best design procedure would be to utilize both of the above mentioned methods.

An initial design can be selected based on empirical rules, and further refined by computation involving analysis and simulation as followed in the CAE approach.   This procedure is complex because it involves two fundamental types of activities; information handling and solving.   This can be made easier if an expert-like system is developed by making use of the techniques from Software Engineering (SE), Data Base Management Systems (DBMS), Operating Systems (OS), Analytical Modelling (AM), and Artificial Intelligence (AI). The material to follow explains the working of an intelligent apprentice system.

8.3 Die Design Using Expert Systems

An expert system is one that is capable of reasoning, drawing inference while performing specified tasks, as well as readjusting itself to new situations.   To understand fully the set up of an expert system in die design, the conventional die designing procedure for extrusion dies is defined briefly.

8.3.1 Conventional Extrusion Die Design

The procedural components in extrusion die design are shown in Fig. 8.2.

In conventional extrusion die design, the designer initially has to consider parameters such as desired shape along with shrink factor of the material, temperature of the extrusion process, etc..   Next, he takes into account the press capacity, press tool arrangement, and the properties of the metal being extruded.   The extrusion load can be estimated (see Chapter 6) using an empirical relationship or an analytical modelling package.   The load calculation can be refined using a Finite Element package, as well.   At each step of the design process the design engineer has to recheck calculations and selections he made previously in order to come up with the right design.

The design engineer, an expert in his field, makes all inferences and decisions regarding die design as shown in Fig. 8.3.   Based on the design objectives, and by making use of empirical, analytical, or Finite Element Analysis processes, the design engineer arrives at an acceptable solution.

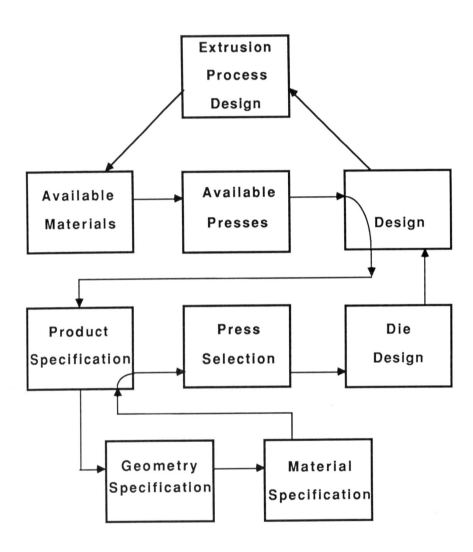

Fig. 8.2 Procedural components in extrusion die design[1]

   The engineer also has to decide on the number of cavities and their position in the die. In addition, the designer has to decide on the die land at various locations at the die exit. The design procedure defined above involves tedious and repetitive work to accomplish a correct design.

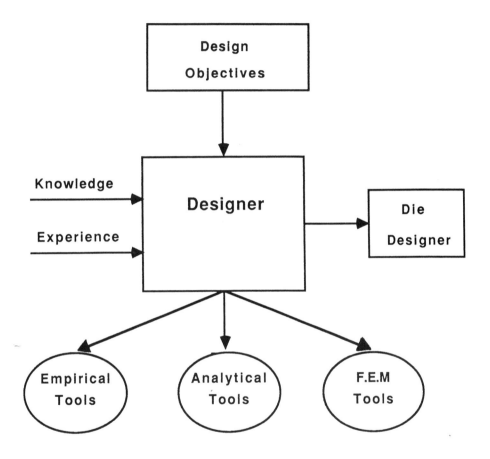

Fig. 8.3 Role of engineer in die design process

8.3.2 *Extrusion Die Design Using an Expert System*

As discussed earlier, the expert-like system is an intelligent system for prompting and aiding the design engineer in his task of finding effective solutions to complex problems. The roots of an expert system are derived from artificial intelligence (AI); which is the simulation of human intelligence using computers. The use of AI is two fold:

(1) The inference process in developing a design (problem solving).
(2) Retrieving, handling, recording and processing information during the design, and implementing decisions.

The design process can be made easier if an intelligent system is developed by making use of the techniques from

(1) Software engineering (SE) for firing of rules and data flow algorithms, and access information that the engineer or programmer might have.
(2) Data base management system for storing and retrieving project information. Furthermore, the DBMS contains the knowledge base, i.e. the domain of facts, beliefs, designers' perspective, and analytical solutions to problems.
(3) The operating system (OS), which would integrate and develop an interface monitor that will allow exchange of information from the data base or from other knowledge based libraries.

Fig. 8.4 shows the basic structure of an expert system. This figure, in contrast to Fig. 8.3, shows that the "thought process," which is essentially an inference device, performs the function of a designer. The operating system makes it possible for the inference device to communicate with a data base or with the design engineer.

Software Engineering (SE) is the heart of an expert system. As the name implies, it is a software developed for the expert system that controls and runs the inference device. The inference device has algorithms built into it to make decisions. The firing order, or approach to a problem, is thus engineered by the data flow algorithm.

The data base may serve as a useful instrument for the designer or the inference device to analyse, correlate and coordinate their work. The work of the designer, such as the number of die cavities in a die, their placement and die land determination is performed by the inference machine using the data base as its source.

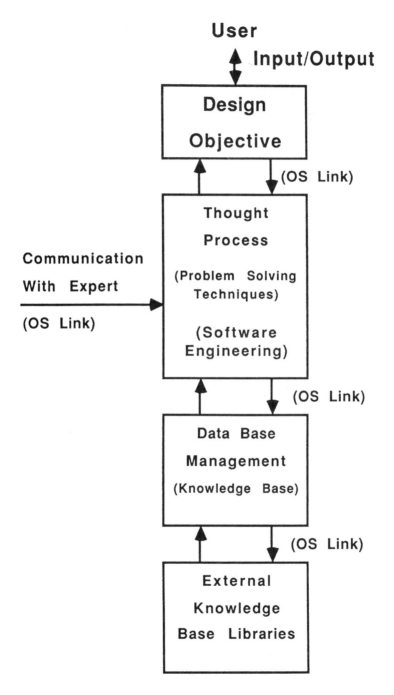

Fig. 8.4 Basic structure of an expert system

The OS develops an interface between the inference device and the user, expert, and other data base libraries, as well. It is possible, with an expert system, to operate without an expert in which case the user runs the systems and all steps from design to manufacturing are executed by the inference device, making use of the data base libraries.

8.4 Expert Systems in Present Use

Success of any design depends not only on analytical methods but depends heavily on an experience base. Recent work on the CAE approach to extrusion of "difficult-to-extrude" materials reveals that the build-and-test methods are not feasible for extrusion of new aerospace alloys (DORAIVELU et al.[3]). To overcome these difficulties, a prototype Intelligent Apprentice System, TRIAD, is being developed by J. RAMANTHAN[3] and associates to exploit the power of existing analytical techniques and heuristic rules in extrusion die design.

TRIAD, an engineering approach to artificial intelligence, is an acronym for TRee-based Information Analyzer And Developer[3]. TRIAD is a meta environment with a knowledge base of methods. In the TRIAD approach, the engineer is the problem solver with the task of identifying a design.

TRIAD synthesizes, within a framework, practical techniques from Software Engineering (SE), Data Base Management Systems (DBMS), Operating Systems (OS), and Artificial Intelligence (AI). Software Engineering techniques in TRIAD support information organization and perform global control functions and access global information in order to answer queries that the engineer might have about the project information. Data Base Management System techniques have been used for storing and retrieving project information while, Operating System techniques have been integrated within the TRIAD environment to develop an interface monitor which will allow problem solving tools to exchange information. As stated earlier, Artificial Intelligence is used in developing the thought process and for handling information.

The knowledge base incorporated into TRIAD for extrusion die design includes factual information on presses and materials, scientific information on materials and extrusion process, design rules based on heuristics and scientific fundamentals, formulas, empirical relationships and various design parameters, weak solving agents such as slab analysis (see Chapter 6), and information on existing software tools and other applications to support problem solving.

The design criteria and knowledge base are incorporated in TRIAD using two approaches; as part of a methodology, and as fragments invoked by TRIAD using integration tools. For example, the design criteria for press selection have numerous and complex relationships among them and require a large number of repetitive calculations. It would be tedious and time consuming to develop fragments or subroutines using conventional programming techniques. Hence, these criteria are incorporated into TRIAD as part of a method. For the other cases, such as the location and optimum number of openings in a die, compensation from thermal shrinkage, and die land length, etc., various software tools making use of scientific fundamentals and analytical techniques, such as STREAM[3], SHEAR (VEDHANAYAGAM[4]), MIS (GOPINATH[5]), and ALPID (OH, et al.[6]), are integrated into TRIAD as fragments. These software tools are also used to carry out some steps involved in design methodology. STREAM is a die design package capable of generating various die shapes based on the user's input, such as die length, billet diameter, product cross-section, and type of die. It makes use of innovative concepts for mapping the product geometry onto the billet geometry to determine the material paths in streamline die design. The coordinates generated by STREAM are used for generating a 3–D wire frame model of the EDM electrode. SHEAR is an interactive CAD and graphics package and is used for shear die designs. MIS (Materials Information System) and ALPID (Analysis of Large Plastic Incremental Deformation) are used for selecting the optimum working conditions and to perform simulations. These programs[3] are integrated into a closely connected network as shown in Fig. 8.5.

The methodology incorporated in TRIAD consists of the following steps for the selection of press and die type.

1. Specification of product shape
2. Specification of the material of the product
3. Specification of the application
4. Selection of the press/presses
5. Selection of die type

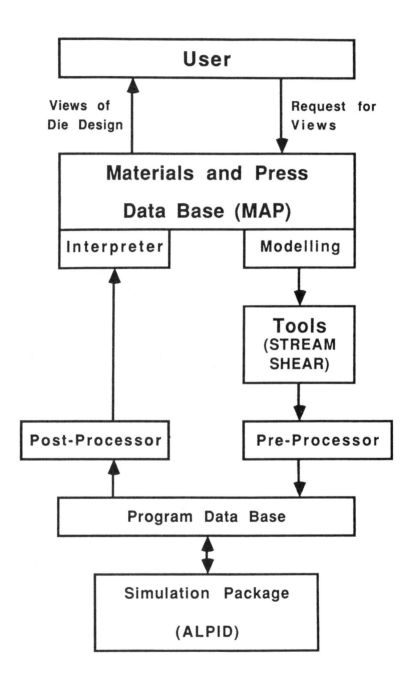

Fig. 8.5 An expert system for extrusion die design

During these steps, the cross-sectional area, perimeter and volume of the product, centre of gravity and circumscribing circle of the cross-section of the product are calculated invoking the fragments of the STREAM package. These values, together with material specification (MIS) are used to determine which press should be used for the extrusion process. While selecting press/presses, the system constantly checks whether it is within the permissible load and controllable ram speed of the press being used and within the limit of diameter and length of the press container.

8.5 Future of CAD/CAM of Dies

By looking at the advances made so far in CAD/CAM of dies, it is easy to conclude that more and more industries will start using CAD/CAM techniques for the design and manufacture of dies for their particular needs. CAD/CAM, coupled with Finite Element Analysis, expert systems, and Artificial Intelligence systems of the future, has the potential to improve die design and manufacture, improve product quality, increase productivity, reduce lead time, and bring down the overall cost of manufacture.

In the future, the concept of Expert System can be used to integrate distributed work-stations into a total conceptual design system managed by a global intelligent system for factory wide optimisation. One advantage of such a system would be its ability to control the growth in the ratio of indirect labour to direct labour. This is mainly because a single engineer will now have control over many conceptual design systems, all having intelligent-interfaces for resource sharing. Thus, the design engineer will be able to investigate many different "Net-Shape" designs, processes, and materials based on having specialized knowledge at his finger tips. The user will be able to select the best method available for satisfying the functional requirements of the part to be produced by Net-Shape processing.

There will be more integration of design, analysis, manufacture, control, and inspection functions using a common data base. In this distributed processing approach, data handling will be simplified and data storage will be reduced considerably. The expert systems which will provide guidance in making decisions could aid engineers in creating new forming processes, new die designs, and new pre-form designs. The development of Artificial Intelligence for metal forming and die design could very well be the foundation for the "next stage of computer aided analysis," which will eventually replace the techniques of CAD/CAM and finite element analysis used today.

REFERENCES

(1) GUNASEKERA, J.S., DORAIVELU, S.M., RAMNATHAN, J., "An Expert Like System For Die Design And Process Selection", *Proc I.E. Aust, International Computers on Manufacturing Engineering, New Castle*, Australia, Aug 1986, 81-87

(2) GUNASEKERA, J.S., GEGEL, H.L., MALAS, J.C., DORAIVELU, S.M., MORGAN, J.T. and GRIFFIN, G., "Computer Aided Engineering Approach To Metal Forming", *Presented at the second International Computer Conference And Exhibition (ASME), San Diego, California 1982 and published in "Computers in Engineering", ASME,* New York, 1982, 58-62.

(3) DORAIVELU, S.M., GUNASEKERA, J.S., BARKER, D.R., GEGEL, H.L., MALAS, J.C., PRASAD, Y.V., SRINIVASAN, R., RAMANTHAN, J., LI, C., "Development of an Intelligent Apprentice System for Extrusion Die Design and Process Simulation", *Proc. ASME Int'l Computers in Engineering Conference, Vol 11,* Boston, 1985.

(4) VEDHANAYAGAM, A., "Computer Aided Design of Extrusion Dies". *M.Sc. Thesis,* Ohio University, March 1985.

(5) GOPINATH, S., "Automation of The Data Analysis System Used In Process Modelling Application". *M.Sc. Thesis,* Ohio University, June 1986.

(6) OH, S.I., LAHOTI, G.G., ALTAN, T., "ALPID- A General Purpose F.E.M. Program for Metal Forming", *Proceedings of NAMRC XI, State College*, Pennsylvania, May 1984.

APPENDIX

APPENDIX 1: CASE STUDIES IN CAD/CAM OF DIES
STREAM - An interactive die design package

A-1.1 Introduction

STREAM is a software system consisting of three packages for the modelling and design of shaped extrusion dies. Although there have been other software packages available for the design of extrusion dies, STREAM is considered to be the only software package capable of designing dies for re-entry product shapes. The package is fully interactive and user-friendly. The user needs no prior knowledge of computer programming or advanced die design technology in order to design extrusion dies - STREAM prompts in simple English commands and very often the user has to type 1 or 2, or Y(YES) or N(NO). The product geometry may be entered interactively through the keyboard, and can also be read from a data file.

A-1.2 Capability

STREAM can be used to design the following types of die geometries (or shapes):

1. Straight - converging die
2. Convex - extrusion type
3. Concave - drawing type
4. Parabolic
5. Cubic streamlined (based on radius)
6. Streamlined (based on area)
7. Constant strain rate
8. B-spline (under development)

Other die shapes (for example SIGMOIDAL) may be included by writing appropriate subroutines.

The following product geometry can be handled:
1. solid product geometry, round, with convex and re-entry geometries - STREAM 4.3 and STREAM STSQ
2. hollow product geometry - STREAM 4.4
3. multi-hole product geometry - STREAM 4.5

Three levels of geometric data are stored in STREAM:

a)   Product geometry, which can be typed through the keyboard
using STREAM or using a digitiser attached to the computer.
STREAM also offers two kinds of radii calculation of the product
geometry, one is a 3-point approximation, and the other is a 5-point
approximation. For larger radii, the latter one can be applied to
obtain a smoother corner or leg radius. Moreover, the user has an
opportunity to use the mapping coordinates directly to avoid
repetitive keying-in. All product geometries and mapping geometries
may be stored and retrieved using STREAM or CUTTER (CUTTER
is a software package for the CAM of the dies designed using
STREAM).

b)   Graphics compatible geometry, can be used for viewing the
geometry of the die. The data file is compatible with the popular 3-
D graphics package called "MOVIE.BYU" developed by Christiansen
and Stephenson of Brigham Young University, Utah. STREAM is
also readily interfaced with INTERACT/INTERPRO32 workstations
made by Intergraph. The die geometry can be displayed with or
without hidden lines, with colour shading and smoothing, and at
different angular or axial positions.

c)   A Programming Tool or Numerical Control (NC) compatible
geometry, is a data file containing the 3-D coordinates of all the
points of the die geometry stored either along splines or across
splines.

A-1.3 Method

STREAM is based on the most advanced die design
technology. It uses a newly developed mapping technique (based on
the Stokes Theorem) for the design of dies for complex re-entry
product sections. The conventional die design concepts developed by
various researchers, notably NAGPAL and ALTAN[1], and
GUNASEKERA and HOSHINO[2], cannot be used to design dies for
re-entry product sections.

Die design consists of mapping sections of the billet on to
sections within the product on proportional area basis. Thus, points
on the perimeter of billet can be mapped on to corresponding points
on the perimeter of the product ensuring the same extrusion ratio is
preserved within each sector. Thereafter splines (of any geometry)

can be fitted from the billet to the product to define the surface of the die.

The estimation of the ram force, stress, strain and strain rate distribution is based on the slab method. This provides approximate but adequate results for the selection of the press and other variables. The length of the die, which can be used to minimize the extrusion force, is still a user input variable. However extensive physical and analytical modelling (using FEM) at the U.S. Air Force Material Laboratories has shown that for good results with Al alloy powders with SiC whiskers, the ratio of die length to billet diameter (L/D) of about one should be used for extrusion ratios of up to about 20. Larger extrusion ratios would require longer die lengths.

A-1.4 Application

STREAM can be used for streamlined die design with a variety of I/M alloys (steel, Al, titanium, etc) and Powder Metallurgy (P/M) alloys with or without whiskers. It is particularly useful for round to very complex geometry extrusions with either single or multi holes and for hollow products. STREAM is considered the only software package capable of designing dies for re-entry product shapes starting from any arbitrary shaped billet and/or multi-hole dies and/or extrusion of hollow products.

A-1.5 Examples of the use of STREAM

To run stream type "@STREAM", which produces the following menu:

```
****************************************************************
*                   STREAM VERSION 4.0                        *
*                                                             *
*                                                             *
*  THIS IS AN INTERACTIVE AND USER FRIENDLY                   *
*  PACKAGE FOR COMPUTER AIDED DESIGN OF                       *
*  EXTRUSION DIES - FOR ASYMMETRIC PARTS                      *
*                                                             *
*                                                             *
*  STREAM CAN BE USED FOR:                                    *
*                                                             *
```

```
*                                                                    *
*   [1] STRAIGHT CONVERGING                                          *
*   [2] CONVEX - EXTRUSION TYPE                                      *
*   [3] CONCAVE DRAWING TYPE                                         *
*   [4] PARABOLIC                                                    *
*   [5] CUBIC STREAMLINE                                             *
*   [6] THIRD ORDER AREA BASED STREAMLINE                           *
*   [7] CONICAL/STREAMLINED                                          *
*   [8] CONSTANT STRAIN-RATE                                         *
*                                                                    *
*   ALSO,                                                            *
*                                                                    *
*   THE OUTPUT PRODUCT GEOMETRY CAN BE USER                         *
*   SPECIFIED.  THE AVAILABLE OPTIONS ARE:                          *
*                                                                    *
*   1.   SOLID PRODUCT GEOMETRY (CIRCULAR BILLET)                   *
*   2.   HOLLOW PRODUCT GEOMETRY                                    *
*   3.   MULTI-HOLE PRODUCT GEOMETRY                                *
*   4.   SOLID PRODUCT GEOMETRY (ARBITRARY SHAPED *
*        BILLET)                                                     *
*   5.   EXIT                                                        *
*                                                                    *
*********************************************************************
```

The user can select the options he wants by typing the option number or exit by typing "5". Each version can also be executed separately by typing "RUN ST43", or "RUN ST44", or "RUN ST45" or "RUN STSQ".

<u>Re-entry Product Shapes - choose option #1, STREAM4.3"</u>

Input the x and y coordinates of the product cross section. Node 1 of the product cross section should come from a point on the billet which intersects the positive y-axis, as shown in Figure A-1.1a and A-1.1b. Note the orientation of the hexagon. Fig. A-1.1a has only 6 nodes whereas Fig. A-1b has 7 nodes because the starting nodes has to correspond with the y-axis. As for "L" section and "T" section (Fig. A-1.2, A-1.3, A-1.4, and A-1.5), the mapping of the billet into the product geometry will be displayed and the user has an opportunity to make small adjustments to the mapping coordinates to facilitate subsequent manufacture of the die by avoiding possible undercutting (Fig. A-1.5). A typical run session is given at the end of this appendix, with the resulting graphic output (Fig. A-1.6 and

A-1.7). Recommended graphics terminals are Tektronix 4000 series, terminals that can emulate Tektronix 4014, INTERACT or INTERPRO32. Round to round extrusion dies can also be designed by using STREAM 4.3 (solid product geometry). Fig. A-1.8 and A-1.9 illustrate perspective views of the die geometry with or without hidden lines.

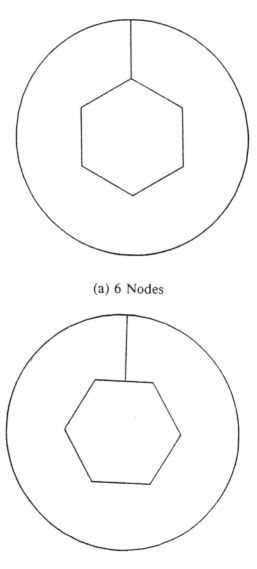

(a) 6 Nodes

(b) 7 Nodes

Fig. A-1.1 Orientation of product shape

Appendix 1

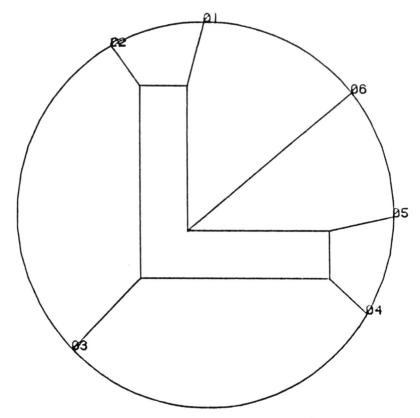

Fig. A-1.2 Mapping of billet into product

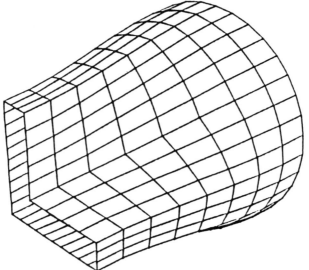

Fig. A-1.3 Geometry of "L" shaped die

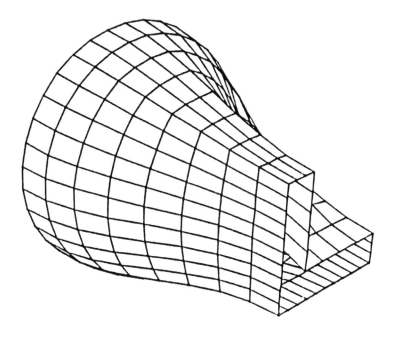

Fig. A-1.4 "L" shaped die - different rotation to show
the other side

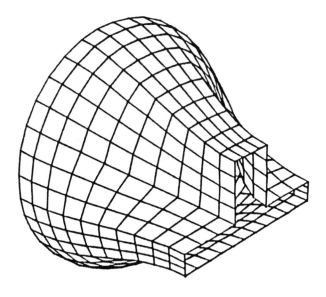

Fig. A-1.5 Geometry of the "T" shaped die

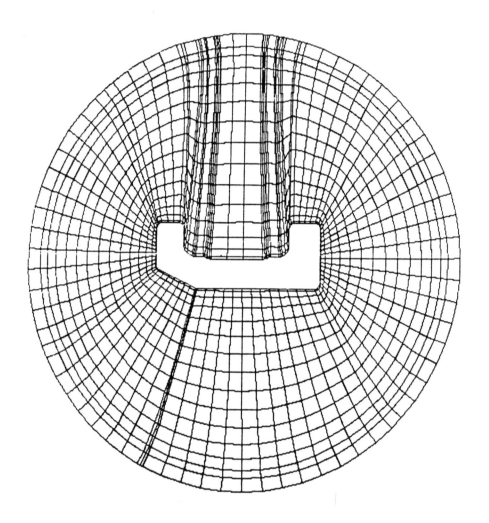

Fig. A-1.6 Graphic output from STREAM

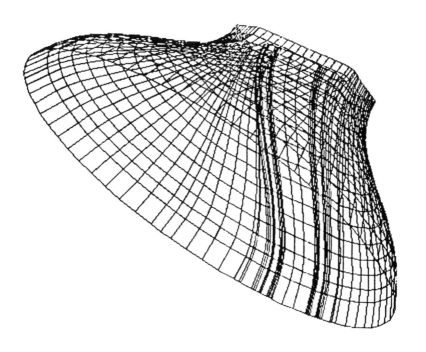

Fig A-1.7 Graphic output from STREAM

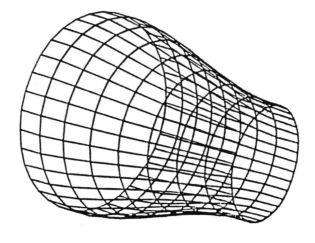

Fig. A-1.8 Round to round extrusion die (with hidden lines)

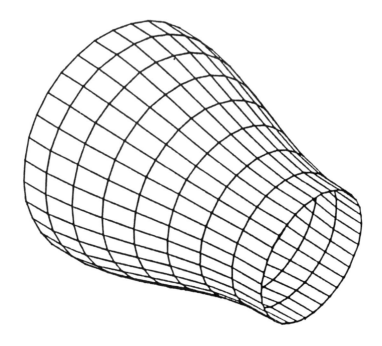

Fig. A-1.9 Round to round extrusion die
(hidden lines removed)

Hollow Products - choose option 2, STREAM 4.4

This program can handle products with round, convex or re-entry shapes. Hollow products can be extruded using either mandrel or piercer. The purpose of mandrel or piercer is to form the hole in the product. They are inside the die, either attached to the ram (mandrel) or at the die exit (piercer). The product geometry is specified in the usual manner. In principle the procedure and logic in the development of this program follows that of STREAM 4.3 the differences are in the product and hollow geometries. To find the centroid, the subroutine "CENTROID" can be modified accordingly.

Multihole Dies - choose option 3, STREAM 4.5

Product-round, convex or re-entry shapes. The procedure for die design is similar to previous cases - except for the billet section shape. The design starts by considering the number of holes in the die and dividing the die and billet into the same number of sections. Start specifying the coordinates of the product starting at the top (and in anti-clockwise order). Mapping proceeds for one sector of the billet. The die can be manufactured by EDM using similar electrodes. Cross sectional areas, extrusion ratio, extrusion force are computed exactly as the other options.

<u>Solid Product Geometry (Arbitrary Shaped Billet)</u> – choose option 4, STREAM STSQ

This program can handle all the above mentioned complex products. This program can design complex streamlined dies starting from an arbitrary shaped billet or a preformed billet.

<u>Common Feature</u> to all the STREAM versions is the radii calculation. When digitising the x, y coordinates of the product or hollow cross section nodes the user can also specify radius at that particular point. The program then approximates given radius by 3 or 5 points. When a sharp corner is required, the input radius is 0, and other than 0 for rounded corner.

<u>Latest Development</u> in STREAM is, in addition to the 3 and 5 point approximation, a 9 point approximation can also be specified. The user now also has the flexibility to have either 3, 5 or 9 points at a particular corner (which is also user specified) depending on the radius of the fillet. A billet diameter optimization option is also incorporated which optimises the same on the basis of minimum ram force and minimum ram pressure. The user then can specify a compromised diameter.

A-1.6 STREAM Sample Run

$ @STREAM

```
*****************************************************************
*           STREAM VERSION 4.0                                 *
*                                                              *
*                                                              *
* THIS IS AN INTERACTIVE AND USER FRIENDLY                     *
* PACKAGE FOR COMPUTER AIDED DESIGN OF                         *
* EXTRUSION DIES - FOR ASYMMETRIC PARTS                        *
*                                                              *
*                                                              *
```

```
*  STREAM CAN BE USED FOR:                                    *
*                                                             *
*                                                             *
*  [1] STRAIGHT CONVERGING                                    *
*  [2] CONVEX - EXTRUSION TYPE                                *
*  [3] CONCAVE DRAWING TYPE                                   *
*  [4] PARABOLIC                                              *
*  [5] CUBIC STREAMLINE                                       *
*  [6] THIRD ORDER AREA BASIS STREAMLINE                      *
*  [7] CONICAL/STREAMLINED                                    *
*  [8] CONSTANT STRAIN-RATE                                   *
*                                                             *
*  ALSO,                                                      *
*                                                             *
*  THE OUTPUT PRODUCT GEOMETRY CAN BE USER                    *
*  SPECIFIED.  THE AVAILABLE OPTIONS ARE:                     *
*                                                             *
*  1.  SOLID PRODUCT GEOMETRY (CIRCULAR BILLET)               *
*  2.  HOLLOW PRODUCT GEOMETRY                                *
*  3.  MULTI-HOLE PRODUCT GEOMETRY                            *
*  4.  SOLID PRODUCT GEOMETRY (ARBITRARY SHAPED               *
*      BILLET)                                                *
*  5.  EXIT                                                   *
*                                                             *
***************************************************************

ENTER THE NUMBER OF OPTION FOR DESIGN >>>> : 1

***************************************************************
```

STREAM VERSION 4.3

THIS IS AN INTERACTIVE PROGRAM FOR COMPUTER AIDED
DESIGN OF EXTRUSION DIES FOR ASYMMETRIC PARTS.
DEVELOPED BY SUPER TECHNOLOGY INTERNATIONAL

STREAM CAN DESIGN THE FOLLOWING TYPES OF DIES

     [1] STRAIGHT CONVERGING
     [2] CONVEX - EXTRUSION TYPE
     [3] CONCAVE DRAWING TYPE
     [4] PARABOLIC
     [5] CUBIC STREAMLINE

[6] THIRD ORDER AREA BASIS STREAMLINE
[7] CONICAL/STREAMLINED
[8] CONSTANT STRAIN-RATE

****

DO YOU WANT TO CHOOSE UNITS (Y/N)

======> N

NUMBER OF SECTIONS ALONG DIE LENGTH ?

======> 15

LENGTH OD DIE ?

======> 11.5

DIAMETER OF BILLET ?

======> 30.16

DIE SURFACE DEFINITION
TYPE 1 STRAIGHT CONVERGING
        2 CONVEX - EXTRUSION TYPE
        3 CONCAVE DRAWING TYPE
        4 PARABOLIC
        5 CUBIC STREAMLINE
        6 THIRD ORDER AREA BASIS STREAMLINE
        7 CONICAL/STREAMLINED
        8 CONSTANT STRAIN-RATE

======> 7

COORDS. OF PRODUCT GEOMETRY
TYPE 1   IF INPUT IS MANUAL
     2   FROM DIGITISER
     3   FROM PRODUCT GEOMETRY DATAFILE
     4   IF PRODUCT GEOMETRY IS A CIRCLE
     5   IF MAPPING IS ALREADY PERFORMED

======> 3

NAME OF DATAFILE WITH PRODUCT GEOMETRY COORDS.

======> PJR

OPTION FOR DESIGN OUTPUT
    1 MOVIE FOR TEKTRONIX/COMPATIBLE
    2 INTERGRAPH FOR INTERACT/INTERPRO 32

======> 1

DO YOU WANT TO VIEW PRODUCT GEOMETRY ? (Y/N)

======> N

MODIFY/CORRECT ANY NODE ?
TYPE 1 IF YES
OTHER NUMBER IF NO
FIRST CLEAR SCREEN / FOR TEKTRONIX TERMINAL

======> 2

TYPE 1 TO FILE PRODUCT GEOMETRY COORDS.
    2 OTHERWISE

======> 2

DO YOU NEED RADII CALCULATION ? TYPE (Y/N)

======> Y

CORNER AND LEG RADII DEFINITION
TYPE 1 FOR 3-POINT TYPE
    2 FOR 5-POINT TYPE

======> 2

DO YOU WANT TO VIEW PRODUCT GEOMETRY (WITH RADII)
TYPE (Y/N)

======> N

MODIFY/CORRECT ANY NODE ?
TYPE 1 IF YES
OTHER NUMBER IF NO
FIRST CLEAR SCREEN / FOR TEKTRONIX TERMINAL

======> 3

TYPE 1 TO FILE PRODUCT GEOMETRY COORDS.
    2 OTHERWISE

======> 2

DO YOU NEED RADII CALCULATION ? TYPE (Y/N)

======> N

****

TRANSFERRING PRODUCT CENTROID TO BILLET CENTER

IF PRODUCT HAS TO BE MOVED IN X OR Y DIRECTION

ENTER X AND Y DISPLACEMENTS

IF NOT ENTER 0,0

****

======> .342 -.469

****

MAPPING OF BILLET TO PRODUCT

ENTER MAPPING PARAMETERS

NEGATIVE AREA PARAMETERS - TYPICAL 0.1

PERIMETER BASE PARAMETER - TYPICAL 0.1

EXAMPLE .5 .5 SEPARATED BY COMMA OR SPACE

****

======> .02 .02

TYPE 1 TO VIEW MAPPING
   2 TO VIEW AND FILE MAPPING
OTHERWISE TYPE ANY OTHER NUMBER

======> 3

DO YOU WANT TO PRINT PRODUCT COORDS. AND ANGLE
TYPE (Y/N)

======> N

PLEASE INPUT THE FINENESS FACTOR FOR
INTERPOLATION OF THE BILLET GEOMETRIES.
FACTOR OF 1 GIVES AN INTERPOLATION OF 10 DEG.
FACTOR OF 2 GIVES AN INTER, OF 5 DEG. AND SO ON.
CAUTION : A VERY HIGH NO. MIGHT CAUSE THE
DIMENSION STATEMENT TO GO OUT OF RANGE, AND THE
PROGRAM MIGHT FAIL

======> 3

ENTER SEMI-CONE ANGLE OF THE DIE

======> 30

ENTER THE LENGTH OF CONICAL PART

======> 1.5

****

X-SECTIONAL AREA OF BILLET	=	713.9835
X-SECTIONAL AREA OF PRODUCT	=	30.3842
PERIMETER OF PRODUCT SECTION	=	33.4848
EXTRUSION RATIO	=	23.4985
VOLUME INSIDE DIE	=	3362.9617
TOTAL SURFACE AREA OF DIE	=	1008.4644

****

TYPE 1 IF FORCE CALCULATION REQUIRED
    2 OTHERWISE

======> 2

TITLE OF MOVIE COMPATIBLE OUTPUT FILE-START WITH
    'M'
    TYPE 0 FOR NULL SPECIFICATION

======> MSAMPLE

MOVIE DATA IS MSAMPLE

TITLE OF APT COMPATIBLE OUTPUT FILE-START WITH A
    TYPE 0 FOR NULL SPECIFICATION

======> 0

DO YOU WANT TO RUN MOVIE (Y/N) ?

>>>>> : Y

<MOVIE SYSTEM DISPLAY>
<READ GEOM FILE> MSAMPLE
<READ: 1 PARTS; 2416 COORDINATES; 2265 ELEMENTS.>
<READ DISP FILE>
<READ FUNC FILE>
<PREVIOUS RANGE:>
< -15.076 <X< 15.080 -15.077 <Y< 15.080 0.000 <Z< 11.500>
<ORIGIN MOVED TO: 0.002 0.002 5.750>
<DISTANCE TO ORIGIN: 105.55, ANGLE: 28.00, ZMIN: 0.10,
ZMAX: 211.10>
< 1 PARTS WITH ELEMENT LIMITS:>
  12265
>> DRAW

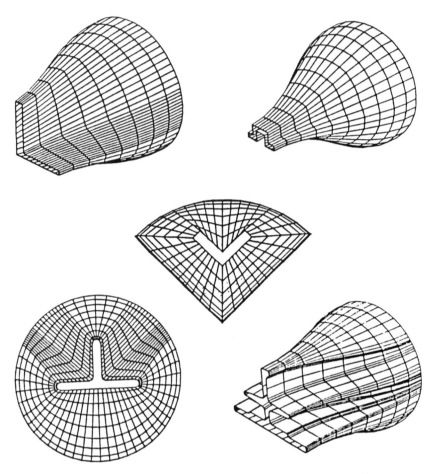

Fig A-1.10 Some examples of die surfaces generated
using STREAM

REFERENCES

1. NAGPAL, V., ALTAN, T., and GAGNE, R., "Computer-aided Design and Manufacturing of Dies for Lubricated Extrusion Shapes", *Journal of Mech. Working Tech.*, 1977, **1**, 183-201.
2. GUNASEKERA, J.S., and HOSHINO, S., "Extrusion of Non-Circular Sections through Shapes Dies", *Annals of the CIRP*, 1980, **29(1)**, 141-145.

APPENDIX 2: GLOSSARY OF TERMS USED IN CAD/CAM OF DIES

algorithm: An error-free system or plan for solving a problem or plotting a figure such as an orthographic view.

alloy: A metal composed of two or more chemical elements.

alphanumeric: Consisting of alphabetic and numeric symbols.

anisotropy: Exhibiting different properties when tested in different directions.

APT: Automatic Programming Tool. A language for writing numerical control programs. It is considered to be the CAM industry standard, being the original and most widely used NC language.

ASM: American Society for Metals.

atomization: The dispersion of molten metal into particles by a stream of gas or liquid.

Bezier curves: Curves defined by the positions of their endpoints and by two or more control points. Usually, the control points, other than the endpoints are not on the curve itself.

billet: A hot-worked, solid, semi-finished, square or round product.

blank: A piece of sheet metal that is to be subjected to further forming operation. Powder metallurgy product requiring additional finishing operations.

blister: A raised area on a surface due to trapped gases or lack of adhesion.

blocking: A preliminary forming operation in closed-die forging.

bridge die: A die used in extrusion of hollow cross-sections.

B-spline curves: Curves defined by approximating their endpoints rather than by matching them. The B-spline has continuity of tangent vector and curvature. The name derives from the flexible metal splines traditionally used by drafters.

CAD: Computer-Aided Design. Computer-Aided Drafting.

CAM: Computer-Aided Manufacturing.

casting: Making objects by pouring molten metal into moulds.

ceramic: A hard and brittle material consisting of compounds of metallic and nonmetallic elements.

CL: Cutter location.

CLA: Centre-Line Average. A measure employed for expressing surface roughness. Also called Ra; the arithmetical average.

closed-die forging: Forging with dies that restrict the flow of the metal to the die cavities.

CNC: Computer Numerical Control.

contour: A single closed-loop boundary which encloses an area, as on a contour map.

CPU: Central Processing Unit.

creep: Elongation of a material under stress over a period of time, usually at elevated temperatures.

CRT: Cathode-Ray Tube.

dead zone: Stationary material in a workpiece during metal-working, especially in extrusion.

dendrite: A branched, tree-like crystal structure, usually obtained during solidification of metals.

DNC: Direct Numerical Control.

DVST: Direct View Storage Tube.

EDM: Electrical-Discharge Machining.

electrode: An electric conductor through which an electric current enters or leaves a medium.

extrusion: Forcing of a material through a die to reduce and change its cross-section.

fatigue: Fracture under repetitive stresses.

FEM: Finite Element Methods. The deformation zone in an elastic-plastic body is divided into a finite number of elements that are interconnected by a finite number of nodal points. The velocity distribution is then approximated for each element. Actual velocity distributions and the stresses are calculated from the solutions of simultaneous equations that are developed to represent unknown velocity vectors.

ferrous: Material containing iron, especially with valence.

fillet: A radius imparted to inside meeting surfaces in a part or die.

flash: Excess metal between two dies.

forging: Plastic deformation of materials with compressive forces.

green: Unsintered, as in powder metallurgy. Damp or wet, as in sand moulds.

hardness: Resistance to permanent indentation. Resistance to scratching.

heterogeneous: Involving more than one phase.

HIP: Hot Isostatic Pressing. Process of compaction of metal powders that has essentially 100% density, good metallurgical bonding and very good mechanical properties.

hot shortness: Embrittlement of a metal at elevated temperatures caused by a low-melting constituent segregated at grain boundaries during solidification.

impact energy: The amount of energy required for fracture,

usually measured by Charpy or Izod test.

impression-die forging: The workpiece acquires the shape of the die cavities (impressions) while it is being upset between the closing dies.

inert: Exhibiting no chemical activity; totally unreactive.

insipient: Beginning to liquify or melt together due to fusion/melting heat.

isothermal forging: Forging in which the workpiece and dies are heated to the same temperature. Also known as hot-die forging.

land: A straight section of a die or cutting tool at its exit.

lattice: Arrangement of atoms in a crystal structure.

laser scan: Scanning lasers are most often used for "reading" (analyzing) photographic or electronically generated images. They can also "write" an image directly onto film or the surface of a photosensitive drum.

LCF: Low Cycle Fatigue.

lofting: An interactive graphics technique in which the third dimension of the image is shown by combining two-dimensional definitions, as in elevating the contours of a topographic map to give three-dimensional representation.

LT: Longitudinal Tolerance.

mandrel: A bar on which the workpiece is mounted during forming or machining.

MOVIE.BYU: A widely used, general-purpose three-dimensional graphics and animation package, developed by the Civil Engineering Department at Brigham Young University. MOVIE is a collection of FORTRAN programs which will describe objects in terms of polygonal surfaces. It has many applications in science and engineering and is used by film animation companies to generate continuous-tone simulations.

NC: Numerical Control.

necking: Localized reduction of the cross-sectional area of a specimen subjected to tensile stresses during plastic deformation.

open-die forging: Placing a solid cylindrical workpiece between two flat dies (platens) and reducing its height by compressing it. Upsetting.

pixel: Short for "picture element", although "pixel" is exclusively a term used in raster graphics and not to be confused with a picture element that denotes a primitive in a vector system. A pixel is the smallest resolvable point of a raster image, using approximately two and two-thirds triads of the phosor dot screen.

plasma: Ionized gas.

P/M: Powder Metallurgy.

Poisson's ratio: The absolute value of the ratio of the lateral to longitudinal strains.

polyhedra: Solid or structure bounded by polygons.

porthole die: A multiple-section extrusion die for extruding hollow shapes.

pyrometer: A device used to measure high temperatures by colour comparison.

RAM: Random-Access Memory. Also, a moving member to which a die or punch is attached.

raster displays: Displays that use the RASTER SCAN technique for assembling an electronic image on a screen by drawing a raster of horizontal lines. They are the most popular kind of graphics display. High-quality raster displays can not only show areas of solid colour but can also display vectors that have been appropriately converted (rasterized) to pixel patterns.

raster scan: The generation of a picture on a raster display. In raster scan, the picture is assembled line by line, as, for example, when an electron beam draws a set pattern of horizontal lines on the surface of a phosphor-coated CRT screen.

RST: Rapid Solidification Technology.

R&D: Research and Development.

roll forging: The cross-sectional area of a bar is reduced and altered in shape by passing it through a pair of rolls with grooves of various shapes.

sintering: Bonding of adjacent particles in a pressed powdered material or in a matrix by heating.

slab method: Method of analyzing the stresses and loads in plastic deformation of materials. It requires the selection of an element in the workpiece and identifying all the normal and frictional forces acting on this element.

slip-line solution: Method of analyzing stresses applied generally to plain-strain conditions. The deforming body is assumed to be rigid, perfectly plastic, and isotropic. It consists of the construction of a set of straight or curvilinear lines that intersect each other orthogonally.

SME: Society of Manufacturing Engineers.

STREAM: Streamlined die design computer program package.

strength: The power of resisting force, strain, or stress; durability.

superplasticity: Capability of a material to undergo large uniform strains before necking and failure.

tensile: Capability of being stretched or extended; ductile.

tensor: An element used to denote position within more than one coordinate system. Similar to vector, but with more than one coordinate system.

thermocouple: A device used to measure temperature. An output voltage corresponds to a particular temperature.

turnkey system: A totally integrated system, including hardware, software, installation, training, and maintenance, supplied by a single vendor who takes responsibility for its success. At least, this is the ideal turnkey system, one that a few manufacturers still succeed in providing.

uniform strain: Strain prior to necking.

upper-bound technique: Method of analyzing the stresses and loads in plastic deformation of materials. The overall deformation zone is divided into a number of smaller zones which consist of particles of constant velocity. Although each zone may have a different corresponding velocity, the boundaries between the zones, or between the die surfaces, all movement must be such that discontinuities in velocity occur only in the tangential direction.

viscoplasticity method: Experimental technique developed to determine the strain rates and the stress distributions in the deformation zone. It consists of placing a grid pattern on a flat surface and observing the distortion of the grid after subjecting the specimen to a small amount of deformation.

volatile: Evaporating readily at normal temperatures and pressures.

Von Mises yield criterion: Distortion-energy criterion. One criterion to describe the relationship between the stress value for yield in a general stress system to the yield stress in simple homogeneous tension, written in terms of the principal stresses.

whiskers: Single crystal filaments a few millimeters long and 1. to 10. micrometers in cross-section. Due to their size, they are either free of imperfections, or their imperfections do not greatly affect their strength.

The names of authors are followed by the numbers of the pages where there is a reference to them or to their published work. Bold numbers indicate the pages on which the complete references may be found.